WELCOME TO HELL

WELCOME TO HELL

THREE AND A HALF MONTHS OF MARINE CORPS BOOT CAMP

By Patrick Turley

Chronology Books
an imprint of
History Publishing Company LLC
Palisades, New York

Copyright © 2012 by Patrick Turley

Turley, Patrick.
   From welcome to hell : three and a half months of
Marine Corps boot camp / by Patrick Turley.
      p. cm.
      LCCN 2012941695
      ISBN 978-1-933909-21-9 (pbk.)
      ISBN 978-1-933909-40-0 (e-book)
      SAN: 850-5942

   1. Turley, Patrick. 2. Marines--United States--
Biography. 3. Basic training (Military education)--
United States. 4. United States. Marine Corps--History
--21st century.   I. Title.

VE432.T87 2012   359.9'654'092
                           QBI12-600128

Published in the United States by
Chronology Books an imprint of
History Publishing Company
Palisades, NY

To my father, for setting an example
of unfathomable character, integrity, honor, and selflessness...
One that we could never hope to match, but one we'd
all be better for striving towards.
And, of course, to my mother, for always being there while
forgiving me for not always being there.

Table of Contents

Prologue

THERE ARE MOMENTS OF BLISS AND MOMENTS OF HELL. THERE ARE years of war and years of peace. Ages come and go and within years, timelines are reduced to sentences and dull whispers that are finally blown away with the wind. To what end? We find an answer in the ongoing struggle to find identity in a world with infinite questions and few answers.

We create images of ourselves in our mind, and then, in our nature, shy away from adversity and change. To grow, the change must be accepted and the adversity challenged. Trials are all we have to seek our true identity. Situations arise when the world seems to stand on end with fear and pain ever present, and a split second given for a decision to be made. Will you stand for what you believe or comfortably lie down to adversity, and hope to convince yourself you were powerless to make a stand?

The moment seems eternal. It is a defining moment when reality is forced upon you. All you know and all you trust become crumbling images that no longer comfort. Then you come to face your inner self. The fear is paralyzing. Will you stand and move through the fear? Will you keep driving and never give up? Are you ready to give all that you are to find the rebirth of a life that has yet to find boundaries?. Are you ready to have the old life die and move forth to find that rebirth?

I couldn't sleep the night before.

Smoke swirled before my eyes as I sat on my couch, staring at the television. Cigarette after cigarette burned down to my fingers. I felt a tangled rush of emotion in my body and a torrent of thought poured through my head. I was unable to sort out what I was feeling. I didn't cry. I just watched as the towers fell.

It was now my moment. I made my decision. I was ready to die and find rebirth...

I needed another cigarette.

CHAPTER ONE

The Beginning

November 16th, 2001, Marine Corps Recruit Depot: San Diego

Silently, while the sun beat down on me, I counted my blessings that I was here at the cusp of fall and winter and not during the summer.

It was hot out. Sweet Lord, was it hot out. Occasionally, I would run my tongue from my mouth to wet my dry and cracked lips. They tasted like salt. The sweat had long since beaded up and was now racing down every inch of my body. Without a free hand to wipe it away, sweat fell to my glasses and through my eyebrows to set my eyes afire with a dull, burning sting.

Maybe this isn't the best idea I've ever had, I thought to myself.

We had spent the first two days in a receiving barracks, having our gear issued to us, taking care of our administrative matters and getting medical affairs tended to which included some thick gel stuck in my ass by, what seemed, a very thick needle. .. Derek and I still had not had an opportunity to talk, even though we were in the same platoon and scarcely more than several feet away at any given time. I could take some solace that my best friend, Derek Bruckner, who had also enlisted with me, was probably sharing the same doubts.

We had our trousers rolled up inside-out on top of our boots and the top button of our "Cammie blouse" a camaflouge shirt buttoned to label us as new, or what they termed "first phase recruits". Unbuttoning the top button and blousing your trousers was a privilege that had to be earned. We had signed away our freedoms and our very lives and pledged to defend the Constitution against all enemies foreign and domestic. Even so, we had to earn the right to defend the Constitution.

Now, here we were, about to "pick up" with our company and our Drill Instructors. None of us had any idea what to expect. We waited in formation outside, our C-bags slung over our shoulders. Before us was our barracks, a monstrous three-story building painted an understated yellow with an adobe feel, each floor lined with large, open windows. To the left of the building was a row of three pull up bars, adjacent to them a tall rope dangling from a frame its height rivaling the barracks. Past that was a shallow area of grass, surrounded by a tall barbed-wire fence, and just beyond that, the San Diego airport tauntingly close with constant airborne reminders of freedom.

Recruits were running everywhere and marching to our side. In the distance, you could see them climbing the "Stairway to Heaven" and the "A-Frame" on the Confidence Course, two things that would soon enough become part of my life.

Shouts of "Kill!" arose from a mulch pit where recruits were hip-tossing and choking each other to the ground. Through all of that, and with everything I now owned strapped painfully to my back, I was part of a file of would-be Marines that climbed up to the third deck of the barracks building where we staged our gear on individual footlockers in the squad bay

A cool breeze whipped through the open windows lining off-white walls. It was a barely recognized relief from the overbearing heat but we were all too preoccupied and apprehensive to have any measure of appreciation.

The squad bay was about seventy yards long built to accommodate two rows of fifty beds. On one end near the door there was a large open area that we would come to know, and dread, as the quarterdeck. Beyond the quarterdeck, the squad bay was lined with large metal bunk-bed racks spaced a yard apart and across from it was a small door simply labeled "Duty Hut".

All I could smell was sweat. I felt light headed. I could fly as I let my C-bag fall to the top of the wooden footlocker in front of my rack. We then formed up, moved to the quarterdeck. and sat Indian-style packed in so close my knees touched the thighs of Anderson, the guy sitting in front of me. We were all nervous, but I curbed my feelings by focusing my eyes forward, with my back straight and hands on my knees, straight up like knives, one of the first things we had been taught.

It was about twenty minutes later when they emerged from the Duty Hut. Walking in and sharply turning before us, all in the meticulously trained discipline that we lacked, were four figures that oozed intimidation, each man with skin tightly stretched over nothing but bone and sinewy muscle, the four figures that would now become our Drill Instructors.

The first one was short and his age deceptive. He could have been in his mid-thirties or younger and rough-looking from years of apparent alcohol abuse. A softer lifestyle and past could have given him an almost mousey appearance, but as it was, he looked hard. The next was younger, with skin even tighter over his face creating an almost skeletal mask over sharp features and what could only be described as an evil aura around him. Next another young, larger man who looked like The Rock. They were all wearing green belts. They stood like boards in a line before us, arms back and hands meeting at the smalls of their backs. Their campaign covers were tipped low, casting a shadow over most of their stern faces. They looked hungry. They looked ready to kill us all if they got the opportunity. Then a young, Hispanic, average-sized man with a youthful visage wearing a black belt completed the wall they formed in front of us.

The one with the black belt stepped forward. "I am your Senior Drill Instructor Staff Sergeant Jameson. This is Drill Instructor Staff Sergeant McFadden (the shorter one), Drill Instructor Staff Sergeant Rand (the skeletal one), and Drill Instructor Staff Sergeant Kebler (the Rock). Over the next three months, you will be broken down through severe pain. Through that pain, you will recreate yourself with discipline and we will make your body *strong*. We are not permitted to hit you, and for your protection you must stay one arm's length from a Drill Instructor at all times, or he will see it as a threat and hit you." He paused taking several minutes to look each one of us in the eyes, one by one. "Who here thinks they can take a Drill Instructor?"

In that moment, I was sure of one thing and one thing only... I didn't want to find out. No one else spoke up, obviously sharing my sentiment.

"Very well. If you have a problem, you come to *me*. We do not care about you, but unfortunately, you are our responsibility, so if it's something serious, you come to me." He looked back at his three hungry pit bulls. "Drill Instructors, you've got 'em." He turned to look back at us. "Welcome to Hell," he said, before disappearing back into the duty hut.

Now the others had their opportunity.

As soon as the door closed behind him, my eyes went wide as they broke from their stances and the squad bay erupted in screams. They had distinct sounding voices, rough and broken or more accurately, like you would expect a dead man to talk. They got in our faces, prodding at us with their fingers and screaming in our ears. Between the three of them at a constant yell, and my focus on my posture, most of the yelling was unintelligible. I just sat there, unsure of what to do or say, even unaware of how I got there.

"Get the fuck on line right goddamn now!" Drill Instructor

Staff Sergeant Rand yelled at us. The term meant to line up in front of your footlocker at the POA, or position of attention. We scrambled to our feet, sprinted before our footlockers, and snapped into our position.

They explained to us that the middle of the squad bay was the "Drill Instructor Highway," and anyone caught in that highway would, in fact, die. Then they paced up and down the two lines we formed on each side of the squad bay, waiting… waiting for someone to give in to any impulse. Waiting to catch someone. A fat kid across the way flinched, sending Drill Instructor Staff Sergeant McFadden into a dead sprint, then into a two yard slide and coming to a halt in front of the recruit.

"Oh, so we want to flinch, huh? We want to do our own thing, huh," his eyes wandered to the name-tape on the recruit's cammie blouse before finishing, "Bequet?"

Bequet began yelling "No, sir!" repeatedly.

"We're on our own freaking program, aren't we Bequet?"

Bequet accidentally yelled "No!."

Drill Instructor Staff Sergeant McFadden's eyes lit up. "No, huh? No?! We're drinking buddies now, aren't we Bequet?"

"No, sir!"

"Then what? Are you fucking my sister?"

"No, sir!"

"You're friggin' nasty, Bequet. Why didn't your mother stop feeding your fat, ugly ass?"

"This recruit's mother is dead, sir!"

Drill Instructor Staff Sergeant McFadden paused and gave him a nod. He turned to leave, but then looked back at Bequet. "So that's why she barely moved when I fucked her."

I was standing still, yet I froze, eyes widening in disbelief. I could not believe what I had just heard. *Was nothing sacred here?*

Bequet just stood there in rage and pain, yet paralyzed by fear and uncertainty. There was nothing he could do.

"Bequet, huh? I'll remember that name, fat ass!"

"Aye, sir!"

"No. Aye-aye, sir!" he howled back, strings of spit spewing from his mouth.

"Aye-aye, sir!"

"Louder!"

"Aye-aye, sir!"

"Looouuuuuuuuuuderrrrrr!"

"Aye-aye, sir!"

Needless to say, I wanted to avoid getting yelled at.

They continued down the line, slapping at elbows, screaming over any discrepancy in our position and similarly degrading anyone who "deserved" it. Then they picked the guide and squad leaders of our platoon. Derek was picked to be a squad leader, and I was proud of him.

Then they yelled for us to "form it up outside." When we reached our given destination, they yelled from the balcony to "get on line"... and so the games began. We went back and forth, sprinting up and down three flights of steps at each command, and battling through each other the entire time for fear of being a straggler, until we "got it right" and were quick enough. In reality, they had killed enough time to get us on schedule to eat dinner, or what we quickly came to know as "evening chow."

"Riiiiiiight *face!*" Drill Instructor Staff Sergeant Rand called to us.

"One heel!" we yelled back as our heels collided. It was one of many mnemonic devices used to hammer the proper immediate action into our brains throughout the learning process of "drill" and the rest of our training.

"Forward... *march!*"

"And step!" we chimed back.

There was a learned rhythm and discipline to drill... and we

didn't have it. We marched like shit. All the way from the beginning, "Forward, march!" and our reply of "and step!", some
stepped off on the right foot, others on the left. Between the bobbing up and down of heads and shoulders while "marching" and
the unsuccessful attempts at staying in step, we had warranted all
the pain we could receive that night.

We halted in front of the Chow Hall and it was explained how
Drill Instructor Staff Sergeant Rand would call out, in squad
order, to "attack the Chow Hall."

"Attack" and "kill", the true motto of the Corps.

"One, two, three, four attack the Chow Hall!"

"One, two, three, four attack the Chow Hall, aye sir!" we yelled
back in unison as loud as we could.

"Fuck, no..." he said back to us with a determined calm.
"One, two, three, four attack the Chow Hall!"

Eventually, we succeeded and filed off by column to form a
line outside the door, or "hatch," and our "guide" ran in the building. Naturally, I was third to last by luck of the draw. They
yelled for us to get tighter on each other, or "nuts to butts" as they
called it. I can't imagine a more accurate term. A deep breath
could be considered an act of sodomy. They resumed walking
our line and slapping at our elbows and hands, yelling "tight
elbows!" or "thumbs on your trouser seams!."

"Ears, thirty-nine!" he screamed.

"Open, guide!'

"Ears, thirty-nine!" he screamed.

"Open, guide!"

"You will be seated at deck three, far bulkhead. Does the platoon understand?"

Not really. "Yes, guide!"

"Does the platoon understand?"

"*Yes,* guide!"

"Attack!"

"Kill thirty-seven!" we screamed, thirty-seven being a "brother" platoon in our Mike company.

"Attack!"

"Kill thirty-eight!" Another Mike company platoon.

"Aaaaaaaa-ttack!"

"Kill, kill, kill 'em all!"

We made it inside and through the line. You moved briskly through an assembly line where other recruits served you varying items of gruel through a request of "peas, recruit" or "potatoes, recruit," and then were teased with beverage options containing a variety of sodas. Naturally, water and juice were the only acceptable options. I took my tray and sat down, as fast as I could, with my left hand straight and rigid on my left knee, back erect and heels together forming a forty-five degree angle, and began to eat. No sooner had I taken three bites, than Drill Instructor Staff Sergeant Rand was up.

"Alright, you want to eat slow?" Every sentence they spoke was as if responding to some personal affront. "You're done! Get up, everybody get up! You're done!"

You have got to be shitting me, I thought to myself. I would just have to start eating faster.

We marched back to the "house" and spent the majority of the night with our footlockers "on line," meaning we held that eighty-pound filled wood box straight in front of us. Seconds after we started, arms began to drop. I was one of the last to keep my arms and footlocker straight in front of me, but it was an awkward and heavy-weight. My fingers stung as the metallic handles dug deeper and deeper into bone. My shoulders burned in protest as I struggled to push the box back out in front of me. It wasn't happening. *Would this day ever end?*

The recruit, directly across from me, let his footlocker drop with a crack that echoed in the squad bay.

"What in the fuck?" Drill Instructor Staff Sergeant Rand said slowly as he turned to check on the cause of the commotion.

The recruit bent over and reached to pick his footlocker back up as Rand approached. He had just grasped the handles and lifted it inches off the floor when Rand stomped on it, sending it down from his hands back to the floor with a thundering crack.

Rand just glared.

Our faces were so twisted in the pain throbbing through our purple fingers, that only hindsight noticed the tension building in the room. We never questioned what was going to happen next. We only wanted a release from the pain.

"Alright," Rand began, slow and deliberate as ever, "I was about to let you put your footlockers down, but since recruit Mason, here, doesn't want to hold his footlocker anymore, he doesn't have to. You'll all pick up his slack. Have a seat, Mason. Make yourself comfortable."

Mason stood there, frightened and uncertain of what to do.

Rand's evil voice was almost singing, "I said take a seat, Mason." Mocking him. Mocking us.

"Aye, sir!" he yelled as he sat down, face etched in shame.

My fingers kept changing color, growing darker and darker. I tried subtly to shift my weight around and changing my grip on the thin metal handles.

From somewhere to the left, someone said, "Wait 'till the lights go out tonight, Mason. Then you're mine."

I had other things on my mind.

After what seemed to be hours of holding our footlockers, we were given the command to put them down. My fingers pounded, trying to regain circulation, but I forced them into a fist for the POA.

"Left boot off, right now."

My hands fumbled for my boot laces as Rand slowly counted down, "Ten, nine, eight, seven, six..."

"Right boot off, right now. Ten, nine, eight, seven, six, five, four, three..."

"Cammie blouse off, right now. Ten, nine, eight, seven, six, five..."

"Cammie trousers off, right now." He counted faster this time. "Ten, nine, eight, seven, six, five, four, three, two, one. You should be...?"

"Done, sir!" we yelled in response to the verbal cue, with the trousers still wrapped around an ankle of over half the recruits.

He stood in the middle of the squad bay, arms folded under his chest, and slowly looked us all over. "Okay, you want to move slow. We'll play games, then. Get dressed right now."

I sighed to myself, frustrated as Rand began to count down, again.

"Put some speed and intensity in your nasty, little bodies!" Drill Instructor Staff Sergeant McFadden yelled, emerging from the duty hut.

Night had since fallen. Being mid-November in San Diego, as the sun dropped below the horizon, the heat disappeared with it and "sunny California" didn't seem so sunny anymore. After two or three more cycles of stripping and dressing, we had finally removed our clothing to their satisfaction and as a reward stood there stark-naked at the POA. Trying to ignore the winter wind whipping through the open windows of the squad bay, we continued to stand motionless, staring straight ahead at the recruit across the Drill Instructor Highway from you. Then we filed off into the "head", one side of the squad bay went to the shower with Drill Instructor Staff Sergeant McFadden and mine to the sink area with Drill Instructor Staff Sergeant Rand.

It was the first time I had seen my reflection in what felt like forever. In reality, it had only been a day. It stunned me, for a moment, to see myself like this. The man in the mirror was expressionless, and I returned my own gaze with a blank stare. *What have you gotten yourself into this time?* I barely recognized my own face. It wasn't the shaved head. It was the feeling I got here. I have to admit, though, I looked gorgeous as ever, shaved head or not.

"Toothbrush out, right now. Ten, nine, eight..."

Fingers scrambling to dig through the camouflage "hygiene bag" before me, I had never dreamed that someday I would struggle so hard just to find my toothbrush.

"Toothpaste on toothbrush, right now. Ten, nine, eight, seven... you're brushing your back teeth. Five, four, three, two, one... now your front teeth. Five, four, three, two, one. You should be...?"

"Done, sir!" I tried to gargle my response with a mouth full of toothpaste.

I stood there, with a mouthful of toothpaste, waiting. No command came. I swallowed the mouthful of toothpaste. One of my fellow recruits had decided to spit.

"Fuck, no!" Rand yelled, running forward and knocking him into the sink, his forehead colliding with the mirror and leaving a spider-web crack.

"Did I say 'spit', you nasty pig?! Well, did I fucking say 'spit'?!" Rand was bent down at the waist screaming in his face as he scrambled to pick himself up from the floor, yelling "No, sir!" repeatedly as he tried.

"Then why did you do it?!"

"This recruit... this recruit..." he stammered.

"Because you're fucking stupid, that's why!"

"Aye, sir!"

"No, say it!"

"This recruit is stupid, sir!"

"No. 'This recruit is fucking stupid!'"

"This recruit is fucking stupid, sir!"

The counting never stopped. We shaved the same way. We started with the left cheek, then the right cheek, upper-lip, chin, and, finally, neck. Then it was time to swap to the showers. We

21

ran, sprinting like the Devil himself was behind us... and I assure you, he was. Derek and the others ran past us naked and dripping wet through the narrow corridor connecting the sinks to the shower room. We each huddled by a faucet until the command was given to start the water.

Our shower time was no better. We stood there naked in the open shower room, being told what body part we could wash and were quickly counted while we did so. Rand seemed to take some measure in amusement in commanding us to wash our faces immediately after our asses. To this day, it remains the most degrading few minutes of my life.

We ran back on line, dripping wet and freezing in the wind, shuffling as fast as we could in our shower shoes, while they made their unmistakable "flop" sound as we moved. We put our underwear, now termed "skivvies", back on, still soaking wet, with our green skivvy shirts tucked into the back waist band and got on line for hygiene inspection. Drill Instructors Staff Sergeant Rand and Staff Sergeant McFadden began the inspection.

"Who are you?" Rand asked, stopping in front of me.

So much for trying to avoid getting yelled at. "Recruit Turley, sir!" I yelled at hard as I could.

"Do you think I give a fuck?" he asked.

"No, sir!"

"Then why'd you say it?"

"This recruit said it because this recruit was asked to by Drill Instructor Staff Sergeant Rand, sir!"

He got into my face. "Why don't you save me the trouble next time and say 'Recruit Bitch'?" Then he began walking away.

I should have yelled "aye, sir!" and left it at that. "No, sir!"

He stopped cold in his tracks and turned back around as rage painted his face through flushed cheeks. "What the fuck?"

He started screaming.

That's when I stopped listening. I learned then, that if you

22

yell "Aye-aye, sir!" as loud as you could, repeatedly, they would simply get bored and move on for easier prey. This was a good example.

"Turley, I'm gonna be watching you."

"Aye, sir!"

"Couuuuuuuuuunt... off!"

"One, two, three..." and so we counted off, one recruit at a time, to ninety-six, until somebody screwed it up along the way. I couldn't believe that people who had been working with the numeric system for so long could forget what comes after thirty-seven.

"And ninety-six!" the guide yelled.

Finally, we had successfully completed our count off and were ordered to prepare to mount and finally to mount our racks. At the command of "mount" we moved as fast as possible on to the top of our racks. We lie there at the POA, over the covers, unsure what it was that we were waiting for.

And then we heard it. Taps played softly and solemnly across the base. It was beautiful. In that moment, that's all it was to me. Later, I would realize the severity that the song represented and think of the brave men who had once lain in the same rack that I now did, and the braver men than I that had fought and died for our country. Not tonight, however. Tonight it was simply beautiful. As soon as it began, it was over, and all that remained was exhausted, yet apprehensive silence.

The silence broke.

"I took the liberty to check your footlockers while you were in the head," it was Rand, "and noticed some of you had forgotten to lock them. So, I took the liberty of locking them for you... comma, pause for dramatic intent." A jingle of metal-on-metal echoed through the squad bay as he pulled a string of forty locks all locked together from behind his back and threw it to the back of the squad bay. It landed and slid into the back wall with a crash.

"You'd better have your lock in the morning. Do not expect every day to be even half as easy as this. Training doesn't even start until Monday. If every day was this easy we'd call you the Navy. Tonight, it'd better be so quiet I could hear a mouse piss on cotton. Hit the goddamn lights."

He was right. My body ached, but, degradation aside, it was an easy day compared to what would come and it was time to sleep now. No nightmares would come to me that night. They would come later. Our training would intensify. The foundation of my life would get twisted inside and out through tragedy. But now? Now, it was just time to sleep, but first I had to find my damn lock.

And that's how it went for the next few days.

Two had already given up. They gathered the whole company in formation around the two and gave them one more chance to resume "training." They said nothing. The M.P.s knocked them to their knees and cuffed them, their police dogs barking and growling in the quitters' ears as they were dragged to the police car and taken to the brig. If I'd had any thoughts of trying to quit and leave, they were gone now.

Any empty moments in our training were filled by repeatedly cleaning our squad bay in the most physically agonizing forms possible. The Drill Instructors would close the windows and have us on all fours in what they referred to as "deck toweling" from one end of the squad bay to the other, and being counted down, of course. Our body heat slowly set the room on fire. We did this until our legs were giving out from underneath us, and our cammies were drenched in sweat. My glasses fogged so badly I couldn't see. I'm not sure if this was dedication that kept us all driving forward, or lack of a choice.

In the morning, we would take our four-inch-long, wooden-with-bristles "scuzzbrush" and brush the floor from "bulkhead" to "bulkhead," wall to wall, all the while in a squatting position, and being counted down. It was never fast enough. Never. We'd do our meaningless tasks over and over again, pushing the associated parts of our bodies past failure. Playing along with their games was our only option.

Saturday night, I was woken up to serve my first fire watch. In a boot camp fire watch, you wake up, put on your uniform, clean, and patrol the squad bay for any disturbance for an hour—as always in accordance with the eleven general orders.

The eleven general orders had been our first, of many, tasks of memorization. Failure to remember, as always, resulted in pain. "Pain retains" was another theme we would all grow accustomed to. General order one: To take charge of this post and all government property in view. General order two: To walk my post in a military manner, keeping always on the alert and observing anything that takes place within sight or hearing. General order three: To report all violations of orders I am instructed to enforce. General order four: To repeat all calls from the guardhouse more distant than my own. General order five: To quit my post only when properly relieved. General order six: To receive, obey and pass on to the sentry who relieves me all orders from the commanding officer, officer of the day, and officers and noncommissioned officers of the guard only. General order seven: To talk to no one except in the line of duty. General order eight: To give the alarm in case of fire and disorder. General order nine: To call the corporal of the guard in any case not covered by instruction. General order ten: To salute all officers and all colors and standards not cased. General order eleven: To be especially watchful at night, and during the time for challenging, to challenge all persons on or near my post and allow no one to pass without proper authority.

I did my cleaning tasks as fast as possible and started my patrol with my flashlight, or "moonbeam." In blatant disregard to the "silent seven" general order, I decided to wake up Derek.

"Hey, buddy," I said quietly.

He rolled over and looked up at me. "Hey, what's up?" he said back, still groggy.

"You doing alright?"

"Yeah, that little guy makes me laugh when he slides. He looks like a cartoon character." He was talking about McFadden. I smiled. I hadn't even noticed it, until then. I choked back my laughter.

"Did you hear when Rand said that 'comma pause for dramatic intent' shit last night? I almost bit a hole through my cheeks to stop myself from laughing."

We both laughed at that.

"Hey, I've had enough of this squad leader thing. Tomorrow, I'm just going to fall in with everyone else, they won't even know who I was."

I nodded and we kept talking until my fire watch was over, giving each other whatever support we could. Like so many experiences we'd shared over the years, at least we were in this together.

Sunday, we went to church in an auditorium. I will never forget that day. The priest came out on to the stage and told us to relax. We slowly shot uncertain glances in every direction, only our eyeballs moving, wanting to believe but entirely skeptical. After a minute I sat back and melted into my chair. It felt so good just to sit and allow the constant tension to drift away into at least a semblance of relaxation. I couldn't believe I used to complain about having nothing to do. Now, a moment of nothing-ness was heaven. Even God Himself, it seemed, could only hold the wolves off for an hour because they were back on us too soon, screaming and pushing for us to exit the building faster.

We practiced drill after that. I don't know for how long, all sense of time and reality were distorted into something completely different during my stay in boot camp. We were making progress in drill. We stepped off together and, for the most part, managed to stay in step.

When we made it back to the house, Senior Drill Instructor Staff Sergeant Jameson called us to the back of the squad bay with our "letter writing gear." Running, we quickly carried his chair to the back of the squad bay for him and built a "throne" around it with footlockers to take our positions. We sat there, left leg over right, left-hand left-knee, right-hand right-knee, rigid as usual.

"Alright, gents, relax for a minute. Let it out, scratch your faces. I know you're dying to."

I didn't believe it at first. I thought it was some kind of trick, but others slowly began to and weren't receiving any punishment in return, so slowly I reached my hand up and attacked an itch. I wrapped my arms around my knees and got comfortable.

He called it his "bubble." It was a place where it was only him and us. The three wolves couldn't touch us here. He was our substitute father. He explained that he would discipline us and take care of us and we could only pray for the latter.

"Look, gents. I know this place sucks... I know it. It sucks, but in terms of your lifetime, three months is a blink of an eye, and trust me, it's worth it. We've already had two quitters. Some of you will break, mentally or physically, and others just won't be fit for the Marine Corps. Take a look around. This platoon is your family now. They're all you have. Let's try and pull together and have everyone make it to February Eighth for graduation."

I smiled. It felt good to smile.

"Grab your ink-sticks. You're writing a letter home. Now, write what I say...."

"Dear Mom and Dad,

I have made it to recruit training. I am doing well. I am a member of Platoon three-thousand-thirty-nine. While at recruit training I may receive mail.

When I am successful in becoming a Marine, I will graduate Boot camp on February Eighth Two-thousand-and-two.

I will be sending more information on graduation as I get closer to that date. I need to know if you want me to buy my plane ticket home, because I will have enough money to buy it here.

I will make every attempt to write. Will you please do the same?

I will not come home until I become a United States Marine. I love you.

Love,

Patrick"

I had to sneak the "I love you" in.

"There are only two kinds of people that understand Marines: Marines and the enemy. Everyone else has a second-hand opinion."
—Gen. William Thornson, U.S. Army

CHAPTER TWO

Training

THE THRILL THAT COMES HAND AND HAND WITH THE SENSE OF ADVEN-
TURE is invigorating. Then it fades...

The idea of leaving life as you know it behind, and joining the
most elite and respected armed force today, to travel the world's
exotic destinations, protecting the ones you love, is both romantic
and exciting. Yet, no matter how many stories you have heard, or
how much you have read, it can never be quite what you thought
it would be. When your thoughts betray you, uncertainty sets in
and you lack the will to fight the fear that soon follows.

Five years, I thought to myself. *Five fucking years.*

My contract was for five years active duty, as opposed to the
traditional four. I had never even known what I would be doing
next week let alone for the next five years, and I hadn't even held
a job for longer than six months. I knew all five years wouldn't
be like this, but it was taking orders. It was complete discipline.
It was kill or be killed.

I had been here less than a week and adventure had already
faded.

Thinking, as it usually does, was only making matters worse.

"My dearest Patrick,
I've been anxiously awaiting for you to write and your letter

finally came today. Can't tell you how often I've thought about you and what you are doing and how you are holding up. I'm sure, with your sarcastic attitude, you're getting yelled at a lot.

Dad was in Chile last week and hopped a plane a day earlier in order to make it for noon on Thanksgiving. He's been reading that book on the Marine Corps.

In your letter, you didn't say if Derek is in your group, is he? That would be nice to have a friendly face through your pain.

By the way, how do you look with your new haircut and glasses? You probably don't recognize yourself, huh pretty boy?

We checked our schedule and you should have gone through receiving and a stress class by now.

Nothing else new here, just that we miss and are thinking of you all the time. We're very proud of you and your commitment. Scared and nervous of the future, but very, very proud of you. Dad's a little bummed because he'll be sixty when your five years are up. It would be nice if you ended up getting stationed somewhere close enough we could visit often.

Well, honey, try to keep a positive attitude. I know these thirteen weeks are far from fun, but just try to keep the end result in sight. Can't wait to see my handsome son in his uniform.

Tell Derek hello from us if you get the chance. I'll write again tomorrow.

Love, love and love,
Mom"

November 19th, 2001, Marine Corps Recruit Depot: San Diego

A lot of people had tears streaming down their faces.

It was our first received letter, and our first big shock of displacement from home. I wasn't crying. I had been away from home for years now, and similarly, hadn't cried in years. I wasn't about to start over a letter from home. It made me happy, for the most part. For some others, it added to the intensity of the pain of separation.

I couldn't help but realize all I had taken for granted, now that it was ripped away from me. When I needed something, it was there. When I wanted something, I got it. I started to realize for the first time how much of a spoiled kid I had been. Now, all I wanted was to be someplace else...

At this point, we had earned what was referred to as "square away" time. It was a half an hour before hygiene inspection where we afforded time to shower, shave, and make head calls on our own, and to insure that our uniforms, gear and tasks for the day had been "squared away." Any extra time was eagerly used to write and read letters from back home.

This was square away time.

"Who's got a girl back home?" Drill Instructor Staff Sergeant Kebler asked, smiling.

"This recruit, sir!" most of the platoon chimed in.

I stayed silent.

"Not anymore," Kebler said back, smile broadening. "She spent the week crying to your best friend about how she missed you. By now, he's already gotten into her pants."

The squad bay went silent in thought. My own memories of my past began to race through my head.

"Seriously, dude, why is your ex such a psycho-bitch?"

I looked different back then. I had a goatee, sideburns, and a fair amount of hair that I combed forward and gelled up in the front. Quite a contrast to my current situation. I was bent down, washing more glasses for the bar. Jeremy was my partner. We were the best bartenders there. Personality, tricks, and were what many would find attractive... for the bar, we had it all. I smiled, putting the glasses back on the shelf. "It's not her fault. I'm just that great and she can't let it go. I completely understand."

31

Jeremy laughed. "Right. She keeps calling and hanging up and bringing different guys in because she can't let you go?"

"Of course not. What else could it mean?" I walked to the other end of the bar where a small group of beautiful women still lingered. "Want another, Tammi? On me?" She was a waitress at a restaurant across the street and she and her friends were regulars when Jeremy and I were working. She had shoulder length dark hair, a black tank top and tight jeans. She wore it all well; she was gorgeous, giving us an excuse to comp several drinks each visit. She had come in with several of her friends and we had all made small talk throughout the night. After all, flirting with pretty women was practically in our job description.

"Guys don't buy me drinks," she answered, matter of factly.

I flashed a smile back. "Then you must have a really shitty personality…"

Her face instantly reddened and her friends erupted in laughter. It was almost closing time, so Jeremy and I went back to casually wiping down the bottles and the glass counter-tops.

Several minutes later, Tammi leaned onto the counter by me. "Excuse me, guys. My friend Beth over there is having a party and we were wondering if you guys wanted to come…" she let the question dangle. You wouldn't have known it from my work attitude, but I was more of an introvert and recluse than anything resembling sociable. I preferred to keep my circle small and coveted my alone time. My silence. "I…"

Jeremy cut me off. He was much more aggressive in these situations than I, often railroading me into situations outside my comfort zone. "We'd love to," he said firmly, looking over at me with an emphatic nod.

She smiled and absently put her hand atop mine. "Great, I can't wait."

I caught her hand as she turned to head back to her friends. "Look, Tammi, it really sounds like a lot of fun and I would love to spend some time with you outside of here, but I really should just go home. It's been a long day and I have things I need to get taken care of."

Her smile disappeared. "Like what?"

I shook my head to buy some time to dig for any excuse. "Just some things I've been putting off that I really should get on top of."

Jeremy laughed.

She squeezed my hand and smiled again. "Look," she started, and then her head dropped as she laughed. "I've never done anything like this before, but..." She laughed again and the red staining her cheeks darkened, maybe in realization of the drunk girl cliché she had just spoken. "Maybe I can help...?"

I'm not sure if my eyes went wide, but I clearly remember smiling through that slow stare that comes with weighing the potential implications of words. Jeremy just shook his head and went back to work on the counter-tops.

"Well... I can't really argue with that. Just hang on a minute while we finish up, okay?"

"Okay," she said, absently biting her lower lip. As she turned, she looked back to smile and the world turned to slow motion as her hair fell across her face.

"I hate you," Jeremy whispered to me.

"I hate me, too," I whispered back.

Tammi's friends started laughing as she told them what happened. "Oh my God!" one of them exclaimed, followed by giggles and another friend calling her a "little hooch".

We finished up and headed out to the parking lot. Jeremy immediately put his arms around Beth and Tammi's other friend and turned his head to wink back at me. I smiled back and laughed softly. He was a special breed that took what he wanted.

Tammi slipped her hand into mine, grabbed my arm with her other and set her head on my shoulder as we headed to the car. "Thanks for coming, Patrick."

I stopped and turned to face her. I was adaptable if anything. Eyebrows arched as wide, eager eyes looked back into mine. She slowly bit her lower lip, expectantly. Maybe offering. I smiled back and cupped her face with one hand.

There would be other time to be alone. I was young and the world and life were good. Now was a time for memories.

I leaned forward and kissed her soft lips as I began to run my fingers through her silky brown hair.

"Lights! Lights! Lights!"

I shook my head, forcing myself to immediately shake off the grogginess of morning and push through exhausted and stiff muscles as I jumped from my rack. I grabbed my glasses from the post and popped to the POA before my footlocker.

Another good morning.

It was the same thing every day. It seemed like we only slept for a few minutes, then would wake up and get dressed while we were counted down. Then we would "attack the head," three recruits to a "pisser," or urinal, while we were counted down. Next we would clean the floor, squatting in a duck position with both hands on our scuzzbrush while we were counted down. After that we would rush to the Chow Hall and eat as much as we could in the few minutes we were allotted. Finally, our day would begin.

"Four, three, two, one…"

"You should be!" I immediately realized that it wasn't Rand saying it.

What the fuck? I thought to myself at the same time Rand let those very words escape his mouth.

I knew that voice.

"Who's the fucking moron?" Rand asked.

"This recruit, sir!"

Derek.

"Bruckner…" Rand said, nodding. He took off his duty belt and threw it across the squad bay until it slid to Derek's feet. "Obviously, you want to run the platoon. Go ahead, take it. I'm done with this shit."

Derek looked more than a little confused. "This recruit can't, sir!" he yelled back.

"Bullshit! You want to do my job, well go ahead. Do it!"

I'd like to think Derek could have put it on, stopped the bullshit, and sent us on the road to chow, but I knew if he even touched that belt Rand would have given him a "pile-driver" straight to the afterlife.

"This recruit doesn't have the skills to lead the platoon, sir!" he responded wisely.

Still, I was biting my cheeks hard to keep from laughing at the exchange.

After yelling "aye, sir!" repeatedly, in response to threats on his life from Rand, he fell back in and it was over.

In the small courtyard between the barracks lie concrete troughs with small shower heads evenly spaced a couple feet apart. Clotheslines were strewn across the area. We stood in our camouflage ponchos at the troughs with our laundry bags at our feet.

"Cammie blouse out right now," Rand called.

We obeyed, pulling a cammie blouse from the laundry bag and placing it in the trough before us.

"Water on, right-fucking-now."

We obeyed, as always.

"Scuzzbrush out, right now."

We pulled out the same scuzzbrush we used to scrub the floor daily.

"You should be scrubbing," he called.

A single bottle of Purex detergent slowly made its way through the way to platoon where we were permitted to use a "dime sized" drop before using it to scrub our cammies "clean" with our filthy scuzzbrushes.

When we finished, we hung our clothes on the clothes lines. We would return later to gather them, still damp and probably even filthier than they had been before.

We resigned ourselves to one fact: Our clothes would never be clean. We would wear brown underwear, dirty socks, and crusted cammies throughout our stay.

We were outside the armory now. The idea of having our own M16 had us all excited. We each had our own ideas of what boot camp would be like, and probably none of them were even remotely accurate. This, however, was something all of us had looked forward to. We were going to learn everything about the M16A2 service rifle. We would shoot with this. We were going to learn how to consistently kill another man from five-hundred yards with this weapon.

We lined up alphabetically, and one by one they handed us our new partner.

They were all fucked up. A patchwork of metals that had faded to different shades of gray, but to us, they were the most gorgeous and prized possession we had set our hands to. Cold, smooth steel sloping and bending as a masterpiece of death sent from God above for one purpose: to kill.

We barely had time to soak in the unloaded and highly regulated power that we now held in our hands before we were off to the classroom, weapons held out in front of us.

We filed off into the building, running as fast as we could and filing off by squad into the seats; Rand, McFadden, and Kebler were all behind us screaming like we had just killed their families. We stood there, at the POA, with our new rifles at our sides... waiting.

"Ready... seat!"

Without hesitation, we dropped on our asses, holding the

muzzle of our rifles with one hand, the other hand placed flatly on the corresponding knee. We attended these classes by series. A company was made of six platoons and split into two series of three platoons each, "lead" and "follow". Our company ranged from three-thousand-thirty-four to three-thousand-thirty-nine, our platoon, and making us a part of "follow" series.

I loved these classes. The instructors were by no means nice, nor were they the hell-spawn Drill Instructors that had turned our lives into a Greek tragedy. They were not out to be a filter for the Marine Corps. They were here to teach and to motivate.

The instructor stepped out.

"Good morning, recruits."

"Good morning, sir!" we boomed back at him.

"Good to go. My name is Staff Sergeant Johnson. We all got issued our weapons today, good to go? Set your weapons down on the table in front of you, ejection port cover up."

What the hell is an ejection port cover?

"First thing is first. Your weapon is your new best friend. Never let anyone take it from you. Name it. Love it. It's the only company you're going to have for the next couple months. When you take your PRAC exam, you will have one minute to disassemble, and reassemble the M16A2 service rifle. This is how you'll do it."

So we learned to disassemble and reassemble our weapons. Considering I was lost at "ejection port cover up," I ended up rushing the entire process, not quite sure I had done it right.

Our instructor stood there and nodded as we sat with our newly reassembled weapons. "Stand-by for your Marine Corps history class."

Then the Drill Instructors were on us, yelling for us to get up out of our seats and run back up the aisle out of the building. It was another group "potty break," where we all attacked the head and packed in our involuntarily shameless and standard three-to-a-urinal position. By the time I had gotten my turn, Rand was already calling us back to the class... I was mid-stream. He ran over and started grabbing to pull me away.

I stood there flopping like a fish, fighting him and trying to keep my aim in the urinal, as he yelled, "You're fucking done, Turley!" while I yelled back, "This recruit is not done, sir!"

I won... if it was possible to view that situation as a victory. I finished relieving myself, and buttoned the fly of my cammies as I ran away. Rand stood behind me, jaw clenched and stone faced, staring.

The next class started the same. A good morning, a reply, and an introduction. He was a tall, skinny, black Staff Sergeant here to teach us history.

"Alright, alright, alright, now, let's start with some review. Who was the first female in the Marine Corps?"

"Recruit Walls, platoon three-thousand-thirty-nine!"

"Kill!"

When you answered in class, you popped to the POA, stated your name, and the platoon you belonged to. Your platoon would respond with a "motivating 'kill'", and you tried to dominate the session to make your Drill Instructors happy. Walls dominated everyone. He was always the first to stand, and the first to answer.

"The first female in the Marine Corps was Opha Mae Johnson, sir!"

"Good to go. Give him one."

"Kill!"

"Give him one", meant congratulate him.

"Alright, alright, alright, moving on. Who was the first Commandant of the Marine Corps?"

"Recruit Walls, platoon three-thousand-thirty-nine!"

"Kill!"

The instructors eyes popped wide open.

"The first Commandant of the Marine Corps was Captain Samuel Nichols, sir!"

The instructor's face flexed as he nodded. "Thirty-nine killing ya'll. Drill Instructors thirty-nine is good to go." I almost sighed as I prayed that would be enough to make them happy for the night, but deep down I knew it didn't matter. "Alright, alright, alright. Who was the father of Marine Corps aviation?"

Walls was up before the question was even finished.

"Recruit Walls, platoon three-thousand-thirty-nine!"

"Kill!"

"The father of Marine Corps aviation was... this recruit does not know, sir!"

The instructor smiled. "Sit your ass down, Walls."

"Aye, sir!" Walls said, taking a seat.

One thing I am incredibly grateful for, is not being able to see Rand's face as Walls admitted failure, or as a recruit from three-thousand-thirty-seven stood and gave the correct answer "Lieutenant A. A. Cunningham."

We gave him one and the instructor went on. "Alright, alright, alright. We got a war coming, and we all know who wins the wars. We do. We do the winning, while the Army runs away, and the other two hide in their boats and planes..."

When we ran out of the classroom I noticed my rifle was making a rattling sound as I ran with it.

I'll fix it later, I told myself. No problem. I couldn't fix it now, anyway.

As I ran by, Rand cocked and turned his head at me, then reached out in front of me and wrapped his hand around the hand guard of my weapon. He pulled, and I held it tight.

"What the fuck are you doing?" he snarled at me.

"This recruit is holding on to this recruit's weapon, sir!"

"Let go," he said calmly.

I let go and it softly rattled as he took it from my hands.

The world shifted into slow motion for a second as he raised it to his ear and shook it. It rattled again. The word "shit"

39

slowly pulsed through my mind as he started to break my weapon down and remove the bolt. After taking the bolt out, he shook it and the firing pin fell effortlessly free. I swallowed hard. Rand smiled at me as he squatted down to pick the firing pin up from the deck. Casually, he turned and threw it as hard as he could twenty yards into the bushes outside our squad bay. Then he calmly reassembled my weapon and shoved it back into me.

My world stopped as I grabbed my rifle back from him. *What am I going to do now?*

"I told you I'd be watching you, Turley. You're my hobby, now."

"Aye, sir!"

I didn't know much about weapons yet, but I still knew enough to be certain the rifle wouldn't work without the firing pin... not at all, but I couldn't find it now, anyway.

What a great day....

We marched to the Chow Hall and stacked our weapons out front. I knew I had to clean the Company Office immediately after dinner, so I was unsure about what to do with my rifle.

"Recruit Turley requests permission to speak with Drill Instructor Staff Sergeant Rand."

"No!"

"Recruit Turley requests permission to speak with Drill Instructor Staff Sergeant Rand."

His face twisted in anger. "Shut the fuck up, can't you hear..."

"Recruit Turley requests permission to speak with Drill Instructor Staff Sergeant Rand."

"What?!" he yelled, throwing his hands in the air.

"This recruit is unsure of what to do with this recruit's weapon while this recruit is cleaning the Company Office, sir!" It was a mouthful, but I was good.

"Fuckin' leave it. Your rack mate will grab it, now leave me alone."

"Aye, sir." Bothering him with validity made me want to smile, but I managed to restrain.

Of course, when I finished eating and returned from the Company Office, McFadden was already screaming at me to meet him in the squad bay on "his" quarterdeck.

We were the only two in the squad bay. The rest of the platoon was outside climbing the rope. "So we just want to leave our rifle lying around, huh?"

I was shocked. "No, sir! This recruit asked Drill..."

He got in my face and started yelling. "I don't give a fuck. Drill Instructor Staff Sergeant Rand's been hogging you to himself. It's my time to play games with you, now." I wished I could have wiped the spit off my cheeks.

Enough! I had put up with enough bullshit over the past week to last a lifetime, and now I had to take more for following an order?

I was angry. "Okay, sir," I said quietly, through clenched teeth.

McFadden's face lit up. "Push-ups!"

"Push-ups, okay, sir!" I said and dropped to do push-ups.

And so it began. Every time he named a new exercise, I would respond with "Okay, sir!" instead of "Aye, sir!", and his anger intensified. It may not seem like much, but in the laws of circumstance, it was mutiny. It was my way of saying, "fuck off". It was my way of saying, "I still have my identity". It was my way of saying, "I will not break". It was my way of saying, "bring it."

It was a half an hour of intense sprints and push-ups before he realized that, tonight, I would not break. He went red with anger; his mind was on the same wavelength and he knew what I was doing. He took a step towards me, and I didn't back down. I stood there at the POA, stone faced and proud, like I had won some imaginary battle. His weight shifted and my stomach leapt to my throat as his fist connected. I dropped to one knee, choking

41

back the vomit that fought its way up my throat, from the unexpected punch.

McFadden only grunted and walked away.

I should have known. *One arm's distance.*

I walked back down the ladder well, nursing my still uneasy stomach. Derek saw me and ran over.

"What happened up there?".

"I'll tell you some other time..." I shook my head a little to try and clear my thoughts. "You name your rifle?" I asked, to change the subject.

"Not yet. Did you?"

"Yeah... 'Angel'."

They say there are three deliberate phases to Marine Corps boot camp. They say you are broken down and then built back up. I never thought I could be broken down. I was too strong willed. I had always done what I wanted, when I wanted, and if no one walked with me, then I walked alone. However, now I even had to piss on command for spectators.

I was tired and hungry, and my body ached from head to toe. Still, we moved too fast for me to even notice. There were times when we stopped, however. Hurry up and wait. We moved, at all times, with speed and intensity. We rushed everywhere. And when we arrived, we would wait. We would stand at the POA for Drill, for the Chow Hall, in the morning, at night, and it was then I became all too aware of the painful tightness stomping up and down my nerves.

That sense of adventure was definitely dead, and replaced by the fear of God, Himself. We were being watched constantly and even the slightest deviation meant serious ramifications.

Maybe I was breaking.

Today, I had been pulled away from the urinal while I was still pissing, had my firing pin thrown into the bushes, and punched in the stomach. Of course, the day wasn't even over yet.

Rand was standing there with his arms folded on his chest, in his usual angry and menacing pose. We were waiting for him to speak, yet feverishly hoping he wouldn't.

"Walls, you got a question wrong today."

"Yes, sir!" Walls screamed back.

"You don't care about the history of my Corps, do you?"

"No, sir!"

"Oh, you don't?" Rand said, really slowly.

"Yes, sir! This recruit does, sir!"

"Then why did you say you didn't?"

"This recruit meant..."

"I'll bet your parents meant to use protection! Go hang on the pull-up bar!"

"Aye, sir!" he said, running to the pull-up bar on the quarter-deck, and began to hang.

"Where's Turley?" Rand asked, wheeling around to search for me across the squad bay.

"Here, sir!"

He cocked his head and exhaled sharply. "Don't just fucking stand there. I just fucking called for you."

I ran over and stood in front of him at the POA before yelling, "Recruit Turley reporting as ordered, sir!" I had known there was more to come today.

"You lost your firing pin."

"No, sir!"

"Then what happened to it?"

"Drill Ins..." I cut myself off. Blaming him wouldn't quite have the effect I needed. "This recruit lost it, sir!"

His lips almost gave the hint of a smile. "You know, Turley, losing a part of a government weapon is a serious offense."

"Yes, sir!"

"How the fuck are you going to qualify on the rifle range without a firing pin?"

43

"This recruit does not know, sir!"

"'This recruit don't know, sir'," he mocked back. "Take your ignorant ass to the quarterdeck and 'IT' yourself. You're not even worth my time."

"IT" meant "incentive training", and in layman's terms "physical punishment for little mistakes." Pain retains.

"Aye-aye, sir!" I said running to the quarterdeck and immediately assuming a push-up position in my shower shoes and underwear. I started pushing.

A few seconds later McFadden walked out of the duty hut and looked down at me. "What the fuck are you doing?"

I popped up to the POA. "Push-ups, sir!"

"No shit," he said back and looked at me for a second. "Well... hurry up!"

"Aye, sir!" I yelled and dropped back to the push-up position to continue.

Out of the corner of my eye I saw McFadden look over at Walls for a second. "Bequet!" he screamed.

"Recruit Bequet, aye, sir!" the squad bay sounded off.

"Aye, sir! Aye, recruits! Carry on, recruits!"

"Kill!" The windows rattled.

"Bequet, tell me why I have two recruits on the quarterdeck, while your fat, disgusting, worthless ass is standing on line?"

"This recr..."

"I can't even hear you over your fat rolls slapping against each other. You're friggin' nasty Bequet, and you always will be. No motivation in your fat ass. We'll put it there." McFadden sneered, then nodded. "Start running in place, Baby Ruth."

"Aye, sir!"

"This recruit can no longer hold on to the bar, sir!" It was Walls, still hanging.

"Shut the fuck up!" Rand yelled back across the squad bay.

"Aye, sir!"

Dead silence swept over the squad bay as Rand and McFadden searched for more victims to join us. I continued to do push-ups, Bequet kept running, and Walls still hung.

"This recruit can no longer hold on to the bar, sir!"

"Shut the..."

"This recruit can no longer hold on to the bar, sir!"

"Get down!" Rand was pissed. Well... more pissed than usual, at least.

Walls dropped.

"Touch the back of the squad bay," Rand barked.

"Aye, sir!" Walls said, taking off running.

"Nope, get back."

Walls ran back.

"Touch it."

Walls started walking toward the back, and Rand's eyes lit up immediately. "No, get back."

"Aye, sir," Walls said softly, turning and walking back.

Rand took a step forward and knocked him down with his shoulder. "If you ever do any shit like this again, I'm taking you into the whiskey locker and beating you so badly you get sent home like the bitch you are."

If I hadn't been there doing push-ups I never would have heard. It wasn't meant to be heard... only promised.

"Aye, sir," Walls said back through grit teeth as he picked himself off the floor.

My arms were so tired, at this point, that my whole body shook, and I had created a puddle on the floor from where the sweat dripped off my forehead. I hurt.

The door of the duty hut swung open. "Where's Turley at?" Kebler said as he emerged.

I popped back to the POA. "Here, sir!" I yelled, silently praising his timing. We had started to notice there was a structure to the Drill Instructors that seemed to run inversely proportional to their viciousness. Our "senior" was clearly in charge. Drill Instructor Staff Sergeant Kebler seemed to come next in a position I would later hear referred to as both the "heavy hat" and "drill hat". Drill Instructors Staff Sergeants Rand and McFadden filled the bottom positions called "bulldogs" or "kill hat."

"These came from medical, today," he said as he handed me a glasses case wrapped with a paper prescription and rubber band. Inside were my new BCs. "BC" stood for birth control because no woman could possibly want to touch you while you wore those glasses with the thick brown frames and lenses. "I never want to see those 'Fuck me all day' glasses again, you understand me?"

"Yes, sir!"

"Now get on line!"

"Aye, sir!" I said and turned to run back on line.

Thank you.

Rand watched as I ran past, slowly nodding his head, arms still folded. "I'm still watching you, Turley."

"Aye, sir!" I yelled back as I spun around in front of my footlocker.

Watch me all day, dick. It's bedtime.

"*Mom and dad,*

A lot of people hate it here. A lot of people get scared when our Drill Instructors, combat instructors, or commanders talk about kill or be killed and Afghanistan and the Marines already sent in. Why? Didn't they know what they signed up for and when? They chose the wrong branch. It's the Marines and it's two-thousand-and-one. It's frustrating that some people are that stupid, or how some people are surprised at how hard it is. They're idiots.

Your schedule is bullshit. There is no 'stress class'. I am in Hell.

I've adjusted pretty quickly. I'm still homesick, but I'm doing okay. I would give anything to be home, watching wrestling with some pizza and a couple sodas, dad asleep on the couch, and you reading the paper. You realize what you had, and how much all the small things meant to you, when they get torn away.

I just hope everyone is doing fine back home and before I know it February Eighth will be here and I'll once again get to spend some time with you all.

Thinking of you every hour on the hour,
Patrick"

"Why in hell can't the Army do it if the Marines can. They are the same kind of men; why can't they be like Marines."
—Gen. John J. "Black Jack" Pershing, U.S. Army

CHAPTER THREE

Breakdown

WHEN THE WORLD TURNS UPSIDE DOWN, AND YOU FIND YOURSELF IN Hell, the hardest part is knowing that life is going on as usual for everyone else, and that you belong here, in Hell.

"Patrick,

I was thinking the other day, boot camp is one quarter of the year that you are in a total void, no contact with the outside. It's almost like you're a prisoner of war. Well, that probably cheered you up!

I wish I could do more to help you get through this, but know how much you are growing inside. This is an accomplishment you should take great pride in. I do. I was always proud of you, but to see what you are doing, it really warms my heart.

Dad has a new boss and he's a real asshole. He's riding him real hard, and you can start to notice the stress affecting him. I don't understand why everyone tries to take advantage of his work ethic.

Well, take care honey. I miss you sooooo much. I would love to be a fly on the wall, just to see what's going on in your life. Tell Derek we say 'hi'.

Love,
Mom"

November 26th, 2001

No, mom, you don't want to know what's going on in my life.

Pugel sticks was tomorrow. You put on a helmet, climb in a ring and hit your opponent with a big Q-tip shaped stick, hopefully before he hits you. Considering we don't fight our enemies with sticks anymore, I think they only keep it around for viewer entertainment. At the least, it was a much needed opportunity to let out some pent-up aggression.

McFadden looked up at me, standing before him at the POA in my underwear and shower shoes. "Get on the scale, Turley."

"This recruit weighs two-hundred-and-twenty pounds, sir!" I yelled back. In all actuality, I was down to around one-hundred-and-sixty, but I always had a burning desire to show off.

"Bullshit. Get on the fucking scale."

"This recruit weighs two-hundred-and-twenty pounds, sir!"

He started breathing heavy. "Fuck it, dig your own grave," he said shrugging, and wrote "two-twenty" on my hand in black marker.

I shuffled back to my new rack, which was next to Walls's and waited for hygiene inspection.

"Recruit Turley reporting for hygiene inspection, sir!"

Rand only nodded. He wasn't in the mood to fuck around with me today, I supposed. "Hit it," he said.

"Snap!" I said holding my hands in front of me, parallel to the deck with my head turned to the right, and my elbows tucked tight in to my body. "This recruit has no personal or medical problems to report at this time, sir!"

"Flip."

"Pop!" I flipped my hands to the other side and snapped my neck to the left. "This recruit's rifle serial number is four-five-three-six-seven-four-five, sir!"

His eyes were trained on my hand. "Two-fuckin'-twenty, huh, Turley? You got a death wish tomorrow?"

"No, sir! This recruit weighs two-hundred-and-twenty-pounds, sir!"

I swear I could almost see him start to smile. "Post!"

I spun around, and pulled my shirt from my waist band and put it on. A quick count-off and then we could sleep.

We had been slipping today. Mason had cost us yet another session of group pain, but for tonight, it was over. Taps played as we lie in our racks, and when it ended Rand started talking.

"You all don't get it, do you? You think this is all a little game. You need to start growing up. You're still moving slow, you still lack intensity, you still want to try and fuck around.. This is the Marine Corps. It's war out there, and when the nation's not at war, *we still are.* The government always has a war for the Marine Corps to fight, but you think this is all a game. When are you going to realize you're not at home anymore? When you're watching your buddies' eyes roll back into his head as he dies in your arms? You will have friends die and it might be your fault. Wake up. Hit the fucking lights!"

Having said his piece Rand left for the duty hut to sleep and fire watch had taken over the squad bay. It was Walls next to me. He was tall, blond and looked a little bit like a cartoon character; especially with the goofy look on his face right then.

"Hey, Turley."

"What's up, Walls?"

"You weigh two-twenty, huh?" he said, laughing softly.

"No, I lied. I'm actually seven feet, and a little over three hundred. I just wanted to make sure I won."

He laughed harder now. "Rand sure loves you, doesn't he?"

I smiled broadly and fought back my laughter. "I just think that's how he shows his affection. How could he not? I'm good-looking, athletic, genius…"

"Oh, so you think he likes you deep down?"

"He appreciates people from good stock."

Walls would never let me live down saying I was from "good stock".

"Where you from, Walls?"

"Austin, Texas. What about you?"

"All over." I paused. "What are you going to do when you get out?"

He laid his head back on his pillow and smiled. "Get drunk and hang out with my girlfriend. What about you? Do you have a girl back home?"

I paused again, this time in confusion. "I'm not even sure I know where home is. I was seeing this girl in Milwaukee, but I left without even telling her I joined the Marines." I laughed. "I left a note with her friend."

He laughed too. "That's cold. What was her name?"

"Angel..." The name lingered on my tongue as exhaustion slowly pulled me off to sleep. Unable or unwilling to make a real connection in this world, it didn't remind me of her as much as it did of women in general... and the life I used to lead that seemed so long ago.

Tammi giggled as I pulled my hands away from her body to fumble for my keys. Softly she bit at my bottom lip as I pulled away to open my apartment door. She laughed and wrapped her arms around my waist, kissing at my neck as we drunkenly stumbled through the threshold.

"Hey, dude, I got..." Derek stopped in his tracks when he saw Tammi. He was standing there in his boxers and a Sombrero, holding a nearly empty bottle of Jose Cuervo in his hand, with one of our kittens, one of a pair of unwanted gifts from an ex-girlfriend, perched on his shoulder.

"Please tell me this is just a friend," Tammi said laughing.

I was laughing too. "Tammi, this is Derek, my best friend and roommate."

Derek tipped his Sombrero to her and raised the bottle high. "Partners for life," he said.

"Hi, Derek."

His eyebrows raised and his chin lowered in feigned embarrassment. "Welp, looks like you had a goodnight at work, huh? I think I'm just gonna go put some pants on then."

Tammi's laugh deepened. Derek had a habit of bringing out that raw, genuine amusement in people at any given moment. "I like your friend," she said after regaining her composure.

I laughed back. "Yeah? Right now, I don't. Drink?" I asked as I opened the cabinet and grabbed two glasses.

A lock of hair fell across her face, covering one deep, dark eye. "I want to know more about you. I don't even know your name..."

"Yes, you do," I replied as I opened the freezer and grabbed a fist full of icecubes.

She brushed the hair from her face. "Your *last* name."

"Turley," I said as I grabbed a bottle of whiskey. Always whiskey.

She laughed and softly wet her lips. "Well that's enough for now. Save the drinks. Come over here first, Mister Turley."

"Get the fuck over here, Turley," McFadden screamed from a forming line outside of one of the pugel sticks "arenas."

I was nervous now.

Why do I always have to act like a hard-ass?

They put my helmet on me, and handed me my stick. These guys were huge. I was pretty certain I was about to get squashed. The series commander was walking around and he recognized me from cleaning his office.

"What are you doing, Turley?" he asked me, with a puzzled look on his face.

"Good morning, sir! About to kick some ass, sir!" I said..

He just laughed. Maybe I was trying to convince myself, and

not him, but all too fast the whistle blew, and the match started.

In the match, you wait at your end of the ring and at the whistle you charge in and fight until a "killing blow" is dealt. I took off running.

Adrenaline surged through my veins with the sound of the whistle, and with it everything became slow motion, just like it does before a car accident. Right before we met, I slid back and jabbed one end of the stick in his helmet. His neck snapped back as he made a gurgling sound, and he went down.

It was over, just like that.

I could hear the series commander yelling, "Yeah! Yeah!" as I handed my stick and helmet off to the next guy, and rejoined my platoon to march back to the squad bay.

When we got back in our little bubble, our Senior stood in front of us. He was too pumped to sit in his throne

"That was some good shit, gents.

"I saw some people give out some serious ass whippings today. That's the shit that motivates the hell out of me. Who had fun out there?"

We all raised our hands. "Who won out there?" Almost all of us raised our hands.

He laughed. "You ain't gotta lie, gents. Some people gave an ass kickin' and some got it... it's the way it goes." He stopped pacing around in front of us and sat down in his chair.

"Alright, gents, I want you to hear this from me before you hear it from the 'recruit underground.' A Drill Instructor from thirty-thirty-eight is getting kicked out, because some recruit wanted to open his goddamn mouth when he shouldn't. There's a lot of shit that goes on here that we don't talk about, right?"

"Yes, sir," we said back.

"*Especially* not in letters home. Your families don't need to be more worried than they already are. Now, has anyone here been hit by a Drill Instructor?"

53

I kept my mouth shut and casually glanced over at Walls. We remained silent. And I used the opportunity to itch the back of my neck while I still could.

"Good. Now, you all motivated the hell out of me, so I'm gonna take you to the PT field. After PT, Drill Instructor Staff Sergeant Rand, Drill Instructor Staff Sergeant McFadden, and Drill Instructor Staff Sergeant Kebler are going to have the night off now. You're with me tonight."

Thank you, God.

"Good morning."

"Good morning, sir!"

"I said 'good morning'!"

"Good morning, sir!"

"Good to go. I am Series Gunnery Sergeant Staff Sergeant Holly, and I will be leading you in your warm up exercises, good to go?"

"Yes, sir!"

"No way, good to go?"

"Yes, sir!"

A big, corn-fed, black kid from Louisiana named Johnson was standing in front of me shaking his leg.

Why is he shaking his leg?

It took two exercises to find my answer. We had just gone into the recovery position, the POA renamed in our physical training environment, when a stream started to pour out of his PT shorts and trickle down his left leg.

You have got to be kidding me.

I wanted to say something, but didn't have the opportunity. Kebler was on him in a second and whispered something in his ear that sent Johnson running off the field.

Then Kebler walked over to me, while I was on the ground stretching my right hamstring, and asked, "Did you see that?"

"Yes, sir!" I answered.

"Disgusting, huh? Don't let me walk in it. You better warn me if I get close."

"Aye, sir!"

Then he began continuing his rounds as we stretched, every once in a while coming back and pretending to walk in it until I warned "Careful, sir!"

Rand walked by a few minutes later, close to the puddle.

"Careful, sir!" I warned.

He turned and glared at me. "What did you say? I'll walk in his piss if I want to walk in his fucking piss, recruit. How about I make you sit in it? Wait until we get back tonight. I'm still watching you."

Jesus... "Aye, sir."

We finished our exercises and did a three mile formation run, followed by a few maximum sets of pull ups and sit ups. I was glad I was in good shape when I joined.. The people who fell out of our runs were guaranteed "extra special" attention until the initial physical fitness test. I was a strong runner, though, and stayed in the front with our Senior Drill Instructor, dripping sweat but starting to love it.

Then we sprinted back to our squad bay and began climbing the rope.

Kebler, Rand, and McFadden left, which meant tonight was going to be a good night.

It was then morning came.

"Inspection... arms!" It was Kebler

Rifle manual. One of the hallmarks of the Marine Corps. It was one of the best symbols of discipline. Having the timing to manipulate your weapon, with intensity, in synch with the rest of the platoon was a beautiful thing.

"One!" We jerked the weapon up from our side to the front of our faces.

"Two!" Right hand moved down to the small of the butt stock.

"Three!" Right hand jerks back on the charging handle, locking the bolt to the rear.

"Four!" Right hand pushes the charging handle back in place, bringing us to port arms, where the weapon is held six inches from your chest.

"Five!" The weapon is raised up, at an angle, and "sandwiched" between your arms while you twist your head to inspect the empty chamber for rounds.

"Six!" The weapon is brought back to port arms.

Unfortunately, it was a beautiful thing we hadn't grasped yet. Our timing was all out of sequence and you could hear the moves being executed at all different times.

Kebler was our teacher when it came to Drill. Sometimes we made him happy, sometimes we angered him. This morning, he was not happy.

He looked around at us. "Did anyone think that sounded or looked good?"

Silence.

"Doesn't anyone take this seriously?"

We all stood there, unsure of what to say.

"Very well. We'll learn the hard way. 'Pain retains'. Hold your weapon straight out in front of you, with two fingers on your front sight post, and two fingers holding your charging handle to the rear."

We all did so. It was only seconds before this became increasing painful and difficult. You could begin to hear charging handles sliding back home and recruits fumbling to recover their painful position. My fingers and shoulders began burning and my face twisted in concentration as I fought to maintain my bearing.

"Look at you. The M16A2 service rifle weighs six pounds and it's kicking every one of your asses. Initial drill is only one week away. We're going to lose if you keep this shit up. You're all a bunch of pussies."

56

It was kicking my ass for sure. The pain was becoming unbearable and occasionally my charging handle slid home, but I would quickly recover and resume my agony. We wouldn't get the chance to set them down for another half hour.

"Long time no talk."

Sunday, finally came and Derek and I marched off to the same church and judged our position so we could sit next to each other and talk while the demons were away.

"Yeah," he said back, "we haven't gone this long without talking since..."

"Ever," I finished for him. "My family says 'hi'."

"Yeah, mine too. What did you do to get on Rand's bad side?"

I smiled at him. "He just likes me, that's all."

"He's riding you that hard because he likes you?"

"Riding me?" I said laughing. "I hope he doesn't like me that much."

It was only a few minutes of conversation before church service began, but it was enough for us to feel better.

Derek and I had been there for each other in nearly every imaginable situation. He was there to congratulate me on my countless new half-assed relationships, and again to catch me as they fell and hand me a twelve pack. There were times when we scraped for nickels just to buy a cheeseburger to eat for the day. We held no secrets and trusted each other even with our lives. School, girls, family, work… No matter what we faced, good or bad, we faced it together. This was no different.

"Mom and Dad,

Hi guys. I hope everything at home is going well for the both of you. Things here are okay. It's hardly a vacation, but I think I'm adjusting pretty quickly. I have weird traditions that help me here. Like when a DI says something really funny, I bite my cheeks to hold back from laughing, and then talk about at it

57

night with some new friends or with Derek at church on Sundays.

I think the Marine Corps is so effective for the simple of reason of three months in this place puts something inside you. A small part of you is and will always be pissed off at everything.

Some people had their wisdom teeth pulled the other day and got the night off to sleep in their beds. I looked at them and just thought, 'I wish I got my teeth pulled.' That's how sick this place is.

It's kinda funny. Right now a DI is just ripping this kid to shreds and I'm just sitting here writing you, like it's a world away. It kinda is. Right now, while I write this, I'm with you two, and I feel happy.

I have to go, I need to sleep before fire watch. I love you guys.

Love,
Patrick
P.S. "Don't you... forget about me. Don't, don't, don't, don't..."

"So they've got us surrounded, good! Now we can fire in any direction, those bastards won't get away this time!"
—Lieutenant General Lewis Burwell "Chesty" Puller,
U.S. Marine Corps

Chapter Four

Initial Drill

In LIFE, AS IN CHESS, THERE ARE KINGS AND PAWNS. THERE ARE THOSE that are thrust into positions of power, and those that are forced into servitude. Yet, some of us, from every background, choose to become servants to protect our beliefs, and in doing so, trade in our freedoms and our very lives, to become pawns.

It was apparent that from one man to the next, we came from diverse backgrounds. This would hold true throughout any Marine's enlistment. However, there was one commonality that connected us all, that had driven us into this situation: we all wore a chip on our shoulder. We all had something to prove.

And that chip served the Marine Corps well,

"Patrick,

I got another letter from you the other day. I can't even explain how much it means to me when I hear from you, and how good it makes me feel. Every day I run to the mailbox and check for your letters and if I get one, I read it on the spot. Then, I'll bring it in for your father and at night, we'll laugh about all the stories you've told us and how you're coping.

We're so proud of you.

I'm just really happy Derek is there with you. There's the old saying, 'misery loves company.'

I'm going to go. It's almost ten-thirty and I have to wake up at six. I have a picture of the Bush twins enclosed so you can stare at Jenna and day dream. You'll be in my thoughts as always.

Love,
Mom"

December 3rd, 2001

"Where's my least favorite idiot?" Rand called through the squad bay. "Where's Turley?"

"Recruit Turley, Aye, sir!" my platoon responded.

I popped into the POA. "Aye, sir! Aye, recruits! Carry on recruits!"

"Kill!"

I ran to Rand and came to a halt in front of him. "Recruit Turley reporting as ordered, sir!"

He handed me my firing pin. "Leave," was all he said.

"Aye, sir!" I yelled and ran back to my footlocker, a monstrous weight lifted from my shoulders.

Initial Drill was coming this week. It would be the first big contest among the company, but first came the series inspection.

We spent the night before, when we were supposed to be sleeping, starching and ironing our cammies, hunting for I.P.s, " Irish pennants" or loose threads, and trying to search for any other imperfection the Drill Instructors might find. We were all unsure of what to expect. Life had been horrible here, and it seemed they found yet another way to add to the unbearable stress level we were already exposed to.

We marched out of the squad bay with our M16s and our freshly ironed cammies. We were ready, we thought. We formed up on the other side of the barracks, in the shade on an already freezing cold day. It was December already, and no one had the time to even notice the passing of Thanksgiving. We were given the command parade rest, where we stood feet shoulder length apart, one hand pushing the muzzle of your weapon forward, and the other resting on the small of your back. Our platoon, thirty-thirty-nine meant we were inspected last, so the Drill Instructors began inspecting at the other end of the series, while our extremities began to freeze.

I remember occasionally trying to clench my fist behind my back to try and warm my fingers up. It took a few seconds to even get them to twitch in response, but they finally clenched into a fist and I felt as if I were in Heaven as they began to warm a little. My right hand, however, I was sure was stuck to the muzzle of my rifle.

Hours later of freezing in one motionless position later, and finally the Drill Instructors made it to our platoon. Rand was inspecting my squad.

Out of the eight Drill Instructors in the series, why him?

I concentrated on staring directly to the front, as he stepped in front of each one us and tore.

He came to Johnson, who was directly to my right, and immediately tore into him. After a few minutes of taking insult after insult Johnson started crying, which only set Rand's fire blazing even harder.

My eyes narrowed and I felt a deep seated anger and resentment brewing in my chest, intensifying with every breath. *Step in front of me, you evil bully.* And he did, all too soon.

Rand stepped in front of me and made a "left-face" until we stood eye-to-eye. I clumsily brought my M16 up with my frozen hand and performed inspection arms the best I could as I fought for control over my fingers.

Rand snarled and ripped the rifle from my hands. "What is the birthplace of the Marine Corps?"

"The birthplace of the Marine Corps is Tun Tavern,

Philadelphia, Pennsylvania, sir!" I yelled back as loud as I could, hoping to hurt his ears.

"What was the first amphibious assault by the Marine Corps?"

"The first amphibious assault by the Marine Corps was at New Providence, Bahamas, sir!" *Take that.*

"What is the five paragraph order?" We weren't even supposed to have known that yet, but a few nights before, I was bored on fire watch and studied some new Marine Corps "knowledge".

"The five paragraph order is SMEAC, sir! Situation, mission, execution, administration, logistics, and command, sir!"

Rand was pissed. "You fail!"

Bullshit. I wanted to smile, because I knew I had won this round, but I stayed stone-like and kept my bearing. He tried to shove my rifle into me, but I met his hands with mine and took my rifle back from him with authority through the sting of frozen fingers.

The inspection went on and most were torn to shreds. Especially by Rand. No one "passed". In fact, I had performed flawlessly, yet "failed".

Soon, the inspection was over and Senior Drill Instructor Staff Sergeant Jameson was in front of us, bringing us to attention and gave the order to march back to the squad bay. Our legs, however, had other plans. In the hours we stood in one position, in the freezing shade, our legs stiffened and refused to obey what we asked of them. We managed to move, but it was pitiful and made Jameson angrier.. As we struggled to move, our legs thawed and we sharpened, but the damage from the inspection and the march had been done.

And we were done for.

We were standing on line. Jameson stepped in front of us.

"Ya'll are an absolute disgrace. Everyone failed. Everyone. I've tried being nice. I've been treating ya'll good, but you've mistaken my kindness for weakness."

Bullshit. It was just another excuse to rip us apart, I knew it.

"Well, *fuck you!* Now, you'll all pay the price." Rand, McFadden, and Kebler, walked out to the quarterdeck, stern as always. "Get your motherfuckin' mattresses on line, right now!"

The whole thing?

I sighed as I ran to my mattress and yanked it on line with me as he counted us down. We all made it, thank God.

"Mattresses in the shower room, right now."

We all sprinted as fast as we could with our mattresses on our back, bouncing off of each other as we ran to the shower.

"You should be?"

"Done, sir!" we yelled back.

"You're not! Get back!"

Not finishing in time of course meant repeating the entire situation again.. Balancing our mattresses, with the linen still made on them, we succeeded the second time and stood in the shower room. Kebler walked in and slowly turned on each shower, soaking us and our beds. After a few minutes of disgrace, Jameson called us on line and had us return our soaking wet racks. Then he called for us to get in his "mother-fucking shitters". We ran and all three Drill Instructors attacked, looking for someone to violate the "one arms distance" rule.

When I hit the quarterdeck, Rand turned and saw me, and smiled. He was ready to pounce and put some sort of pain on me that I was not ready to take. I must have had a high school football flashback in the moment. I stepped and turned my shoulders to the left, and as soon as he committed to tackle me in that direction, I pivoted and ran right by him.

Rand pursued easier prey as I disappeared and body checked another recruit. I had "juked" Drill Instructor Staff Sergeant Rand, and smiled as I piled into a stall with ten other people, packed in as tightly as we possible..

Drill Instructor Staff Sergeant Kebler walked in with our guidon, the flag of our platoon, and stabbed it through the toilet, the porcelain shattering immediately upon impact.

"That's what this platoon means to me. You're all a bunch of shit-bags."

It hurt. It cut to the bone. Our flag, our guidon, represented all our effort and all our pain. Now, there it was planted firmly through the porcelain toilet.

We heard Rand's voice next, cutting through our thoughts and disappointment. "Get on line, right now!"

We sprinted and slid in front of footlockers, hoping to please them so this ordeal could end.

"Unlock your footlockers, right now."

We did so. We were moving faster these days, so most of our tasks were accomplished before the end of a reasonable count down.

"Dump them out in front of you, right now."

Fuck, no.

I was pissed now. I grabbed my footlocker and dumped all my belongings, in this new world, out onto the floor. Then Drill Instructor Staff Sergeant Kebler came by with a bottle of liquid detergent and dumped it all over our belongings. We wouldn't have time to rinse off every item we owned until night which meant another sleepless night.

It hadn't even been a month yet.

After lights out, we all crept out of our very damp racks to clean our gear and few personal effects. I held one of my canteens in my hand and reminiscing, flipped it to catch it behind my back and back again until I held it before me. Czarnecki, a small Polish guy, watched and smiled.

"How'd you learn to do that shit, Turley?"

I smiled back. "In my other life, I used to bartend…"

The bar went silent. I flipped the bottle back over my head, caught it behind my back and tipped it back over my head to roll it back over my thumb into a pour. There were a few cheers and claps, but not many, as I topped the drink off with coke and slid it across the bar. Jeremy and I always did "flair", or tricks, when it was slow to help pass the time and potentially increase tips, and so far, it had been slow.

We had a cute a little hostess, at the end of her teenage years, who walked by then, smiling at us as she moved past. We couldn't help but watch her walk away in her skin hugging pants.

"I love the nights she works," Jeremy said to me.

I nodded and softly exhaled. "You have fun at the party after I left?"

Jeremy smiled back at me. "Oh yeah, it got interesting." Then he shook his head at me. "I don't even have to ask about your night, do I?"

I smiled and shook my head. "Probably not, but I'd be happy if you did."

He just laughed.

In the corner sat a thirty-something year old man and a woman drinking whiskey and mudslides respectively. The woman was quietly sipping on her drink through the straw while the man stared at me.

"Another whiskey?" I asked.

"I've got a question for you... she wants to know, not me."

The woman laughed as red began to streak her cheeks. "I do not!"

I shrugged. "I'll do my best. Shoot."

"How does the hostess get into those pants?"

My eyebrows furrowed. "I don't know." Slow or not, I wasn't in the mood for some pervert that mistakenly thought he was entertaining. "Can I get you another drink?"

"She wanted to know, not me!" She slapped his arm and laughed, her face now bright red. At least someone thought he was funny. "Yes, I'll take another."

When I returned, he began his pitch. "So you're pretty athletic with that bottle throwing stuff, huh?"

Still disinterested, I responded curtly, "Just takes practice."

"Wait. We're recruiters for the Marine Corps. Maybe you'd be interested in stopping by sometime to talk?" He most likely found any excuse to compliment younger people and open the door to this conversation.

"I appreciate it, but no thank you."

He wasn't giving up that easy. "You'll be missing out on..."

My patience was wearing thin. "Look, I'm kinda doing the whole school thing and I make some really good money here... having *fun*. It sounds like a great time, but no thanks."

He nodded. "I'll leave my card. Call if you change your mind sometime."

I shook my head, only humoring him to end the conversation sooner than later. "Fine."

Every day here had been the equivalent of being mentally raped. I could only wonder that if everyone knew what this hell-hole was really like, would anyone even join?

Time wore on and the stress of initial drill was coming. We heard rumors about the punishment that came along with second place and below.Yet, we had also heard through the "recruit underground", that we were the favorites and felt confident in our discipline and ability. The Drill Instructors helped maintain that focus through fear, and finally, the day came.

We woke up, ate breakfast, and came back to preparations. The Drill Instructors brought out a CD player and let us listen to music. The diversity of backgrounds gave little room to agree on something as cultural as music, but, without squandering the opportunity, we got pumped up to a mixture of *Godsmack* and DMX as we made the final preparations to our boots and cammies. Before long, we were getting dressed.

I walked to the head, dipped my hands in the water and ran them over my bare head. It was a ritual I initiated when I played football. I would wet my hair before a game and, even though it was under a helmet, I felt better and more confident. I didn't have hair now, but it was familiar and set my nerves at ease.

Derek walked up to me. "Ready, old buddy."

I nodded. "Let's do it."

Kebler marched us out until we were next to the parade deck, and had us gather around him. "Alright, look. I've been watching a bunch of the other platoons and I know you can do this. Senior Drill Instructor Staff Sergeant Jameson may be your Senior Drill Instructor, but you are *my* platoon, you understand that? Now, in a couple minutes we're going to go out there and put thirty-thirty-nine in charge."

We were pumped up, in a zone, then it came. We gathered around on the parade deck, and waited. My palms were sweating on the muzzle of Angel, and then it hit us, Rand's voice calling, "Fall in!"

We ran and began our competition.

Like every competition in life, it wasn't really between the company and our platoon. It was us against ourselves. A simple function of command and execution.

We performed inspection arms flawlessly. All the snaps and pops hit at the same time. I had been moved to the front for my skill at drilling and I could see Jameson in the judges hut, smiling.

We continued to execute as we moved into marching. Our heels sounded like thunder as they pounded into the parade deck beneath us, we flanked, we turned in columns, we turned obliquely on command , and then as soon as it began, "Fall out!" was called, and it was over.

The Drill Instructors were happy as they marched us back the squad bay, and we stood outside... waiting.

After at least an hour, Jameson came back and talked with Kebler for a few minutes, and then stood before us.

"Well, gents. You gave it your all, and I think you did your best, and I think you did the best out of everyone out there today. The judges didn't agree. You took fifth," second to last, "and I think that's bullshit. So, I'm not gonna fuck with you. You all did good, don't let anyone tell you otherwise."

It was depressing. We were amazing out there, but for some reason we only beat out one other platoon. I found out months later the platoon we beat came in last because a recruit pissed on himself on the parade deck.

What did we do wrong?

"Mom and dad,

Got your letters and can't tell you how supporting and helpful they are. Thank you guys so much for being here for me.

You know how anxious I've been about this upcoming initial drill, right? Well, today we went out there and did our best... we took fifth place, or second to last. I don't ever want to talk about it again, but I thought you might want to know what the outcome was.

I've been here about a month now, and we had all tried so hard, and today we saw that it was all for nothing. Not very uplifting, but I guess all I have to look forward to is February Eighth anyway, and that's what keeps me pushing forward everyday. Getting to see you two again.

Well, it's time for me to go. I look forward to hearing from you again, and you two never leave my mind.

Love,
Patrick"

"I come in peace, I didn't bring artillery. But I am pleading with you with tears in my eyes: If you fuck with me, I'll kill you all."
—Marine General James Mattis to Iraqi tribal leaders

68

CHAPTER FIVE

Confidence

PEOPLE ARE OBSESSED WITH QUESTIONS WITH WHICH THERE ARE NO definite answers to. What is the meaning of life? Why are we here? Where do we come from?

I can thank the Marine Corps for teaching me that I don't really care. I don't care. I only care about the people I love, and appreciating the moments I have with them. Moments that can be ripped away, like they had been to me.

"Patrick,

I hope your Drill Contest went well, I have my fingers crossed for you, and I'm sure you guys will get what you deserved.

Dad and I are getting ready to have a Christmas party for everyone at work, so I've been trying to get a hold of caterers but of course dad wasn't sure what we should order and waited so long, it's almost impossible now, and of course he's off in Columbia, but that's how it goes, I guess.

I guess complaining to you is the wrong person. I can't even imagine what you're going through, and wish I could, though I'm sure I wouldn't be happy with how you're being treated.

Work is still really getting to your father. I've never seen him so frustrated with his job before. I'm starting to get a little worried.

I just wanted to take a minute and remind you how much we care and can't wait to see you in February. We love you.

Love,
Mom"

December 10th, 2001

"And seventy-eightttttttttttttt!" roared the voice of Rand.

Thirty-thirty-nine was down to seventy-eight recruits.. Twenty less. No one I had concern for was missing. We were all in this together. Circumstances forged a tighter bond with some but many had caused the group undue pain, and I couldn't feign concern to watch them leave.

"Listen to you girls. Seventy-seven Mariah Careys and one fucking Whitney Houston."

The guide actually cracked a smile this time.

"You know, guide," Rand said, approaching him, looking predatory as ever. "They say uncontrollable smiling is a sign of homosexuality. Are you... wait, never mind. I can't ask, so I guess we'll never know."

I bit down on my cheeks harder than ever, and I think a smirk still managed to escape my efforts to hold bearing. Having a rack near the quarterdeck had its obvious disadvantages of being closer to notice, but it also came with unexpected privileges in the form of hearing more amusing "private" conversations.

"Anyway," Rand said turning around. "Seventy-eight of you to go, then I can go home. Who's next? Mason?"

"No, sir!" Mason called back.

"Yeah, right. You'll break, Mason. Then it'll be, 'and seventy-sevennnnn'."

It was a week stuck in limbo.

Initial drill was over, swim week began next week, but what now? The answer was simple, and just like every week, "what now?" was answered with "too much." Still, initial drill was over, and with it we were no longer "first phase" recruits as we entered the "second phase" of our training. Our top button came undone and our boots were now bloused instead of folded into cuffs. It sounds like nothing, but it's a silently respected status symbol among recruits, but still didn't compare to the respect shown to the recruits who returned from "up north" at Camp Pendleton, known instantly by the hair on their heads.

Monday morning we were on the Confidence Course. I wasn't afraid of heights but there was something about being thirty feet in the air, and running across logs spaced three feet apart and then leaping in the air to grab a rope on the A-frame that made me uneasy.

Out of all these experiences and self-revelations, one thing stood out above all the others. The Confidence Course. The situations I found myself in, doing life-threatening things simply because of a man behind me screaming threats, was amazing to me. I ran through the Confidence Course like a possessed demon, beating out every partner I had and using my nervous energy generated by uneasiness to propel me forward. Then I hit the monkey bars...

I made it four or five bars in, and then while reaching higher for another, fell to the ground. Rand, who had been supervising, and barking for us to move faster, just stood there with his jaw dropped, as I ran back to the beginning and tried again. I fell again.

Rand walked away, I guessed to laugh without us being able to witness his bearing break, and turned back. He looked at me, arms folded in his traditional pose. After a few seconds, he actually cracked a smile. "You've got to be fucking kidding me, Turley. You've taken everything so far, and been running through this shit, and now you're falling on the fucking 'monkey bars'?! Tiny little kids do this shit! What is wrong with you?"

71

"This recruit can't do it, sir!" was the best I could do to explain my hands sliding off.

"Why not?"

"This recruit does not know, sir!"

He shook his head. "Amazing. Fuckin' amazing. Get the fuck out of my face, before I punch you."

"Aye, sir!" I yelled and took off running to the Slide for Life.

The Slide for Life is a thirty foot tower, with a thin cable that extends down over a pool of muddy water and finally to the ground on the other side. You started your climb down with your chest on the cable and facing towards your destination. One third of the way through, you flip off your chest with your legs still wrapped around it and continue your climb underneath the cable. A few yards from the finish, you were to drop your legs and hang, then kick your legs back up to the cable to finish your climb to safety.

I made my way up the ladder, pounced on the cable and began my climb down. After I swapped to the second position, another recruit was able to begin his descent on the same cable. He must have been hesitant about mounting the rope, because once he was on, the instructor at the top of the tower grabbed the cable and began to violently yank up and down on it to make him fall.

Fuck.

By the time I had hit the middle of my descent, the cable was flying up and down at least a yard in each direction as he continued to tug at the cable, and I struggled to hang on. Finally, before I dropped to the third position, I heard a splash beneath me, and the shaking was over. I let my legs fall, and then went to kick back up to finish legs first. The series Gunnery Sergeant was standing there, screaming something about my thumbs.

Who gives a fuck about my thumbs!

I let one arm drop from the cable, holding with only one arm as the cable began to shake again. *I'm gonna fall.* I reached back

72

with thumbs facing the other way, then did the same with my other arm, and finally kicked my legs up, and finished. This accomplishment was met by getting screamed at by the series Gunny for not "paying attention during the brief", but by this point, we had all become immune to screams, easily capable of tuning out the noise like it was a world away. The Confidence Course was done.

I felt good.

We got back to our squad bay, Rand and Kebler immediately began searching for recruits with wet cammies who had fallen from the Slide for Life and tore into them.

Drill Instructors Staff Sergeants Kebler and Rand took us out for drill after they had satisfactorily finished humiliating every last "failure" of the Confidence Course. As we marched to the parade deck, I heard a whisper.

"Turley."

It was Riddle. Riddle was a tall, skinny black recruit from Louisiana that McFadden had taken a particular interest in. Like me, and everyone else, he looked ridiculous in his BC glasses. "What?" I whispered back out of the corner of my mouth, desperate to avoid being caught talking during a march.

"Did a bird shit on my face?"

What? "What?"

He whispered slower this time. "Did a bird... *shit*... on my face?"

I bit on my cheeks to fight my amusement and shot a quick glance to the right. "No."

"Platoon, halt!"

They saw me.

"What is it... Mason?" Rand yelled.

"Recruit Mason requests permission to..."

"Go!"

"This recruit was wondering..."

73

Rand threw up his arms in an exaggerated display of frustration. "You wonder?! The 'wonder years'! I wonder how you'd feel if I punched you in the fucking throat!"

Kebler turned around as a smile began to creep across his face and walked away.

Rand looked over the platoon quickly. "Holy shit, Bruckner! You'd better straighten out that leg before I kick it in like Joe Theisman!"

The attitude of the Drill Instructors were starting to change toward us. The whole ordeal started to shift from senseless abuse to actual instruction... It was either indicative of our entrance into second phase, or I was just getting used to it all.

We went in for our uniform fit the next day, and for the first time held a uniform other than cammies. We were almost giddy as we put our Alphas on, slowly looking around at each other and wondering what we looked like ourselves. And then it slowly soaked in and we started to realize that before long, most of us would be Marines.

Derek came over to me. "What do you think?"

"You look outstanding, buddy." I took my BC glasses off and set them on the table. "What about me?"

"Enough to turn a straight man gay."

We both started laughing as I put my glasses back on.

"You know, every time I see you in those things I laugh really hard... on the inside."

"Thanks."

After we left the tailor, Rand marched us out past the parade deck and left us at the post museum. We split into two groups to take two hour tours.. The tour guide was an old, retired Marine who was nice to us. Mutual respect was something I had not felt in a long time.

We saw weapons, and paintings of battles from the past and heard stories of men with courage we could barely fathom. As we walked around learning more about the events of the Marine Corps history, and less about memorizing facts, I began to appreciate the role they had played in our nation's history, and I began to respect the Corps more and more. I was looking forward to becoming part of it, and maybe being a part of some activity that made it into the museum.

The tour, like everything else, couldn't last forever.

We formed up and began marching but after only a few feet, Rand called "platoon halt", and told Willis he was fired and to fall in the back before he punched him in the throat.

We had, what I called, two equal opportunity squad leaders, since the beginning of boot camp. No matter how bad they were, almost every minority had taken a turn at being a squad leader. Only yesterday, Willis had been placed in charge of first squad, and had already gotten fired.

"Turley, get the fuck up there."

I sighed to myself as I ran to the front and we resumed our march home. I didn't want this.

Back home we hit the showers and Mason had been whistling cadence as he left the shower room, strutting past the duty on the quarterdeck in his towel and shower shoes.

"Who the fuck was that?" Kebler yelled, bursting out of the duty hut during our square-away time, incensed with rage. "What the fuck did I tell you mother-fuckers about whistling?"

"This recruit, sir!" Mason said, immediately taking responsibility for his action.

Kebler nodded and then called for us to bring ten sweatshirts, Gore-Tex jackets and filled camouflage war-bags to the quarterdeck. He then instructed Mason to put them all on, and after being handed a deck towel by Kebler, told to deck towel the squad bay.

It was after we had mounted our racks and listened to Taps that Mason had finally passed out from heat exhaustion and lay unconscious on the quarterdeck as we fell soundly asleep, thankful it wasn't us.

"Seems like you had another crazy night," Derek said to me, Miller High Life in hand..

"You too, by the looks of it," I laughed back at him.

"She seemed like a nice girl. You should introduce her to your mother."

One of Derek's favorite past times was poking at me for reaction. It didn't work this time. I'd become far too accustomed to it over the years. It rarely worked anymore, but when it did, it was worth it to him.

I had been making drinks all day. I grabbed the bottle of Jack Daniels. It was time to make one for myself. "Very nice," I said as I poured the whiskey into a plastic Sesame Street cup.

"So what's next in the life of Pat Turley?" he asked before taking a long drink and finishing his beer.

I held my breath and drank the whiskey straight with a burning swallow succeeded by a bitter head-shake. I grabbed two Miller High Life's from the refrigerator and handed one to Derek. We twisted the caps off and I held my bottle up in a toast.

"I thought we'd get drunk watching a movie until we pass out."

Derek raised his bottle in response and said, "Best plan for the future I've heard yet."

With a clink of the bottles, we drank.

Derek walked over and threw himself on the couch as I walked to the blinking red light of the answering machine and pressed play. *"You have two new messages."*

I walked back to the couch and took a seat next to Derek. We drank in the illumination of the television glow.

"First message: Hey there Pat, it's Theresa. I just wanted to see what you boys were up to tomorrow. A friend of mine is having a party on the East side. Give me a call if you guys want to come."

Absently, I bobbed my head from side to side as the news ran a piece on the winter attractions for the Milwaukee County Zoo.

"Second message: Hi, Patrick, it's Tammi. I just wanted to say I had a great time last night and I'm looking forward to seeing you again, okay? Bye for now, Tiger."

Derek craned his neck with one eyebrow arched, a smug smirk creasing his lips. "Hand me the remote, 'Tiger'."

"Shut up," I replied, handing him the remote. Anxious to change the subject, I said, "Oh! Get this…I had some recruiters from the Marines in today trying to get me to join." I pulled out the card they had left on the table.

"'Staff Sergeant Smoter'," he read. "What'd you say?" he asked as he handed the card back to me.

"What do you think I said?"

"'No'."

I nodded. "Quit my lifestyle. Drop out of school. Take a pay cut. For what? Greg always said joining the military during peacetime was like kissing your sister."

"Greg your dad's friend?"

"Yeah." I looked over at him. "We got a good thing going and I wouldn't give it up for the world."

Derek raised his bottle again and I tapped mine to it. "Amen, brother." Derek turned his attention back to the television where a trainer was working with a polar bear. "Man that looks like fun."

I cocked my head to the side. "The zoo? Let's go."

He looked back, face wrought with curiosity. "It's midnight. They're closed."

I smiled. "…So?"

The Marine Corps Martial Arts program was a wonderful tension reliever. Ever since we picked up with Mike Company, the series would meet twice a week, and the recruits would pair off and begin training.

It would start with "body hardening" which consisted of kicking and punching your partner in his most sensitive nerve endings along the forearms, inner and outer thighs, and stomach. The harder you struck and were struck, the more the nerves were damaged decreasing sensitivity and increasing tolerance for pain. Then we practiced punches, kicks and elbow strikes on the nerves.. After that, we learned hip tosses and various throws, followed by counter and submission holds. Finally, we learned blood chokes.

In a regular choke, you cut off the oxygen supply to the brain and, in a minute or two, rendered your victim unconscious. If, however, you cut off the blood flow to the brain, as in a blood choke, your victim is unconscious in a matter of seconds.

McFadden was there, we hadn't seen him since initial drill, but he was with thirty-thirty-eight. I stood there wondering what was going on when Rand stepped in front of me. He had the last night off, and Kebler put us all to bed.

"It's been a while, you miss me, Turley?" he said sarcastically.

"Yes, sir! This recruit missed Drill Instructor Staff Sergeant Rand very, very much, sir!"

Rand just looked at me. "What the fuck?" He turned to Johnson next to me. "Kick his ass, Johnson."

"Aye, sir!" Then Johnson faced me. "You better kick me good, boy, cuz I used to kick-box and I'm not gonna go easy on you."

It was my turn to go first. I nodded to the bed wetter.

"One!" called out the instructor.

"Kill!" I yelled, pointing my lead foot, and swinging around hard with my striking leg. My foot connected with his thigh a few inches above his knee cap and he went down.

"Damn," he said, picking himself up from the ground. "You don't look like you hit that hard."

"Two!"

"Kill!" He was still trying to get up as I sent him back down to one knee.

"Johnson, just stay the fuck down," Rand said, pushing him to the side and back to the ground. "This is how you do it." Rand walked up in front of me and swung his foot into my thigh.

My knee buckled and I hit the ground.

"Kick me, Turley," his voice was taunting.

Unsure of what to do, I threw myself back to my feet and swung my leg out and gently kicked him back.

Rand cocked his head to one side. "What the fuck was that?" he said kicking me back down to the ground. "Fuckin' kick me!"

All of the frustration from the past month began to surface and fuel an anger that wanted release. I snarled, and kicked back hard. His leg buckled but he stood tall and kicked me back. This time I stood my ground and kicked him back.

We went back and forth, kicking each other and taking our feud to a new level. I had eluded him and shown him what I could do for the past few weeks since he started "watching me", and he had been a thorn in my side since day one. Now, we took our aggression at each other out once and for all.

I had read about the Stockholm syndrome, the emotional bonding with the captor or abuser and I knew deep inside that I was, in a strange way, seeking favor and approval from Rand. The kicking felt better and better and I knew in his strange way he was liking what I could do..

Later, Rand had us formed up outside when a recruit from a different company started to pass behind him. I ran out of formation and pushed the recruit back until he was a yard or two away from Rand.

"'Good afternoon, sir! By your leave, sir!' or some shit, recruit!"

"Good afternoon, sir! By your leave, sir!" the recruit yelled off to Rand, scared as I glared at him, blocking his path.

....

"Carry on!" Rand yelled, and then sent me a curt and cold nod as I fell back into the formation. Stockholm Syndrome.

"Alright, gents. I'm sure some of you have noticed Drill Instructor Staff Sergeant McFadden is no longer with us. He had to go to thirty-thirty-eight because they were down to two Drill Instructors. I know he was a little intense, but he was damn good, and I'm sorry to see him go."

So was I. He made my life Hell sometimes, but damn it he was ours. Thirty-eight didn't deserve him...

"Mom and dad,

Glad to hear everything is going well at home. Hope dad's work situation gets better, I know how it feels to be stuck in a shitty job you don't like. Ha ha!

It's been a fun week. We did the Confidence Course, which made me nervous at first, but ended up being incredibly fun. We also got to try on our uniforms to get them tailored. I look amazingly handsome, of course. We even got to go to the museum, so I'm pretty relaxed.

Next week is swim week, so I'm pretty excited about that. I'm sure they'll find someway to make it no fun, but being in the water again will be nice.

I hope you two are doing great. I can't believe Christmas will be here in a week and a half. I'll be stuck here, but you guys will be with me in a round about way. I love you both tons.

Love,
Patrick"

"Do not attack the First Marine Division. Leave the yellowlegs alone. Strike the American Army."
—Orders given to Communist troops in the Korean War

CHAPTER SIX

Swim Week

"A LEOPARD CAN'T CHANGE ITS SPOTS," AND IT'S SIMILARLY HARD FOR a human being to change. Yet, here I was, growing into something I didn't understand yet. Something I may never fully understand.

Less timid and afraid. Eager to confront and challenge, even in these extreme circumstances.

"Patrick,

Glad to hear you were able to have some fun last week. You don't know how much that helps put my mind at ease. Your great uncle Eddie, died last week. I'm not sure how much you remember him, but he was a great man.

Dad was incredibly happy to hear from you, as usual, and laughed about you both hating your jobs. He's not sleeping much anymore, so I worry, but then again I worry about everything.

By the time you get this you should be starting swim week. That should be a lot of fun for you, you've always been drawn to the water and are a real strong swimmer.

Well, I gotta go meet your father for dinner, so stay strong and I love you.

Love,
Mom"

December 17th, 2001

Swim week, at last. I had been excited about this week Water had always soothed me. Now, it was finally upon us.

The entire company was formed up outside the pool, waiting for our brief by our swimming instructors before we began.

"Turley, can you swim?" Moore asked me. He was quiet and meek, either by nature or by letting the never ending hurricane of stress here slowly chip away at his insides.

"Fuck yeah, I can swim."

He gave me a look that had "I'm sorry" written all over his face.

"Hey Riddle, can you swim?"

Riddle kept staring straight ahead. "Nope." Riddle paused. "But I 'fin to try today."

I couldn't help it. I burst into laughter for a second. It was too funny. I bit down on my cheeks as hard as I could to regain my bearing before being noticed.

"Riddle," I began, now whispering out of the corner of my mouth. "Seventy-five percent of your body is water... so if you think about it, only a quarter of you has to do any work." It was bullshit, of course.

Riddle looked puzzled. "Shit, I never thought of it like that."

"Anyone here had pink eye in the past couple weeks?" the swim instructor called out, walking in front of us.

Nearly everyone had gotten pink eye there, but Rand had already warned us not to raise our hand for anything because we'd be dropped from swim week and forced to drop two weeks behind in Alpha Company. Being dropped back, for whatever reason, was nightmarish fate. Enduring any more time in this place than was absolutely necessary was to be avoided at any cost.

"Alright, everyone get changed and meet in the bleachers by the pool."

We entered the locker room, changed into our PT shorts and walked through a shower spraying freezing cold water at us on our way to the bleachers. Then we had to dress up in a set of wet cammies and boots so big they looked like clown shoes, and then, finally, got our briefing.

I was on top of the diving board. It was only twelve feet, but like every activity I had been in so far, from the Confidence Course to brushing my teeth, I was nervous.

The swimming instructor was standing in front of me with his arm blocking my path. Then he moved his arm out of the way, and I shuffled forward until the front half of my legs were dangling over the edge. "Look down, look up, jump."

I jumped. For the past month, it'd been a constant stream of being yelled at, punished in an extremely creative variety of ways, and stressed out, with no time to clear my mind and ask myself if I were okay. Then it was all swept away. The sounds of screaming were suddenly washed away as I was immersed in the water and gravity pulled me deeper.. A sense of peace swept over my mind as I relaxed and let myself fall deeper and deeper, savoring the moments, a world away from the surface. Eventually, those moments of peace began to slip away as my lungs started to throb for air. Finally, I pushed off the bottom of the pool towards the top to take a breath of air.

"Good God, Turley! Take your friggin' time, too. You better get to the goddamn end of the pool right friggin' now." It was McFadden, he was here with the rest of the company Drill Instructors. In the moment, it was bitter sweet. I missed getting yelled at by him, but it was as aggravating as ever at the same time.

"Aye, sir!"

I should have stayed underwater.

We swam laps back and forth, grabbed rubber rifles and ran through the water with them held above our head. We played dead and had someone swim us across the pool while in flak jackets and Kevlars, swapped them and swam back in the other direction.

I ended up taking WSQ2, the second highest swim qualification, while Derek left with a first class. He had to be dragged underwater in a blood choke by an instructor, fight his way out of it, and swim back to the surface three times, but he did it. When he finished he passed out spread-eagled on the edge of the pool, only to be awakened by the series commander Captain Wiles.

"What are you doing, recruit?"

Derek stood as fast as he could, and then wobbled left and right as he said, "Getting dressed, sir!"

The series commander and our Senior Drill Instructor stood there and laughed at him as he stumbled back to the changing room.

Swimming had been such a second nature activity throughout my life, a suburban summer past time along with barbeques and cookouts. I saw first-hand that it was not a natural or a fun thing for all of us. Water turned some people frantic. One of the recruits in my platoon made it halfway across the pool doing the side stroke when his nose burst into a stream of blood out of sheer anxiety and he became hysterical, with tears rolling down his cheeks, then he started choking on water. Rand grabbed him from the side of the pool and jerked him to the cement before he laid into him.

We tested in our Marine Corps Martial Arts that Wednesday. Our entire platoon went clean, which meant no one failed, and everyone had earned their tan belt. Our Senior Drill Instructor was very happy.

The PFT, physical fitness test, was coming, however. It was the next big event between the platoons in the company, and it was only a few days away.

But for now, we stood on line as our Drill Instructors paced the Drill Instructor Highway, predatory and waiting. Rand came to a halt before me, silently staring like a hunter with lupine eyes.

It felt familiar.

The wolf seemed to stare back at me, cautiously and curiously eyeing me up and down with a determined confidence.

We had broken into the zoo that night as planned, and as we had previously done years before with "Six Flags: Great America." The zoo was off to the side of Bluemound road, an expanse covered in a tall fence. We had parked in a neighborhood across the street and then waited until the road's traffic died down, which hadn't taken too long at around one in the morning. At that point, we had made a mad dash across the road and over the fence, and began our exploration.

Most of the exhibits were closed, but that didn't stop us from enjoying our stay. We were fearless and carefree, or oblivious and stupid. We had a close encounter, with security. The headlights of a jeep came towards us from one of the side paths as we struggled to find our way into the heart of the zoo. I pulled Derek with me for cover behind a snow bank. It passed, and the night was ours.

Derek had climbed to the top of an aviary some twenty feet high, and did his best poses for the camera we had brought with us then we explored.

Eventually we came across the "Wolf Woods." Wolves have always fascinated more than other animals. I admire their intelligence, nobility and structure. It was dark and the exhibit was massive, but before long small groups of wolves approached to investigate what was intruding on their territory.

We stared at each other for a long time. Eventually, the beautiful animal in the front just sniffed and turned to walk away, the others filing off behind, leaving us to ourselves.

I looked to the outside of the exhibit where one of several "Wolf Woods" banners hung on a wooden stake and made my way over to it.

"What are you doing?" Derek asked through a broad smile.

I reached up and began unfastening the banner from the stake. "I'm taking this. I want something to remember."

He just laughed at me. "We'll never be able to forget this night! Only you..."

I smiled back as I finished claiming the banner as my own and quickly rolled it up. "Only you would come with me for something this stupid."

He nodded. "Always."

Senior Drill Instructor Staff Sergeant Jameson ended up being the one to march us to the PFT course. It was here that a large portion of our value to the Marine Corps would be summarized with three exercises: dead hang pull-ups, sit-ups, and a three mile run. Twenty pull-ups earned you one hundred points, one hundred sit-ups in two minutes earned you one hundred points, and running three miles in eighteen minutes earned you one hundred points for a perfect score of three hundred. Every missed point was a point further away from being an ideal Marine, or ideal recruit in our circumstance. Failure was not an option. We fell out and got in line at the pull up bars. There was a Drill Instructor behind each bar, to count for us. I was first in line, and McFadden was counting for me.

I came to the POA in front of the bar.

"Mount the bar and come to a complete dead hang, Turley."

"Aye,sir!" I leaped up, grabbed the bar and hung for a second.

"Begin."

And I began. He counted, "One, two, three, four," and so on as I cranked them out as fast as I could hoping to outrace the exhaustion that would quickly creep into my arm and back muscles.

"Thirteen, fourteen... fourteen."

Bullshit. I knew my chin was clearing the bar, and I was coming to complete hang in between each one. "Fourteen," he counted again. I was starting to get tired. "Fifteen, fifteen, fifteen." My arms were wobbling now, I tried one last time, pulling myself half way up and fell back to a full hang.

"This recruit is done, sir."

"Drop. Fifteen, huh? You could've gotten twenty. I'll be sure to let Drill Instructor Staff Sergeant Rand know about this."

I did do twenty.

We fell in for sit-ups and I pushed myself past one hundred. By the time our two minutes had ended, I had done one-hundred-and-forty-two.

The run was next. The fastest I had run three miles in, at this point, was twenty minutes and thirty seconds. The whistle blew and I was off. It was only a couple minutes into it when I started hurting. It started as a dull cramp in my side, but as I ran it turned into a sharp, stabbing pain. I was determined, however, and I pushed myself forward, focusing on breathing as I did my best to ignore it. My heart was pounding in my chest as my feet pounded the ground beneath me, and then I could see the finish line. It spurred me forward and I pushed myself harder. I felt like my heart was about to explode despite being in great physical shape.

"Nineteen-twenty," they called as I ran in, then slowing myself down and panting for breath. I held my hands above my head as I walked back and forth around where our platoon had staged our canteens and waited for the rest. A few had finished before. Some right after. One by one they slowly trickled in as time ticked by.

"Where's Bequet?" we asked amongst ourselves.

To have a chance at winning, we needed to go clean, and to go clean, Bequet needed to pass the run.

Finally, he came in and we all rushed him. "Did you pass?"

"I passed," he said.

No failures.

We ran back to the barracks and got on line for our PT shower. A PT shower consisted of getting naked, briskly walking through the shower room after the Drill Instructors had turned the water on, running back on line and getting dressed under a countdown. We had gone clean in our second major event, so we thought they'd be happy with us and give an extra minute or two getting dressed.

Kebler burst out of the duty hut and slammed the door behind him. "What the fuck is going on? You went clean in the PFT and now you think you're hot shit, huh? You don't have to move with speed and intensity anymore, is that it?"

"No, sir!"

"Clothes off your body, right now." Over a month of these games and we still had not gotten used to it. It was just as frustrating every time. "Ten, nine, eight, seven, six, five, four, three, two, one... you should be?"

"Done, sir!"

"Assume rack positions!"

Oh God, no.

"Assuming rack positions" meant we stood in between the metal frames of our racks and grabbed a hold of the frame.

"Make 'em float."

"Make 'em float" meant we lifted them off the ground. We had done this several times before when they were angry at us and it always hurt. Yet, we had never before done this in the nude.

It is a memory that is, unfortunately, forever burned into my mind. Knees slightly bent, with all my strength pulling up on the two racks I had my hand on. Fully tensed, you're unable to look anywhere but to the front of you, where across the squad bay,

Czarnecki was doing the same. Muscles flexed that I did not know existed. My jaw clenched tightly as my face twisted to echo the strain this placed on my thighs and shoulders. I just thank God I was in the front of the rack and not the back, their view must have been even worse.

"Put that shit down!" It was Jameson.

The racks hit the ground with a thud as we all stood, relieved that it was over if only for a moment.

"You went clean, gents. Which gives us a good chance of winning. All you motherfuckers are going 'up north' together. Good to go. I'm proud of you. I just got done talking to the series gunny and he noticed that we went clean for MCMAP and the PFT, and he thinks you're all pretty locked on, so he's putting you on maintenance for Team Week. That means, there won't really be any Drill Instructors around, but it also means you have more unsupervised time to get in trouble. Don't fuck this up, gents. I'm happy with you right now, don't fuck it up."

"Mom,

Swim week was a blast. Yeah, they found ways to suck the fun out of it, but water is water and I enjoyed myself. Derek ended up getting a first class, and there's a crazy story behind that, but I'll tell that to you later.

I have a whole bunch of funny stories from this place that I can't wait to tell you, but I'll have to. Derek and I will even reenact a few of them for you guys and his parents at graduation. Graduation. . . it's starting to seem closer now. We go into Team Week, now, where our contact with Drill Instructors is minimal. Then we go 'up north' where time should fly by so fast, before I know it, it will be graduation.

I really want to thank you for taking the time to write as often as you do. You don't understand how supportive and motivating it's been for me to hear from you guys. Being pulled

89

away from everything in your life really has a way of showing you what's important in life, and you guys are what's important to me.

> *Love,*
> *Patrick"*

"My only answer as to why the Marines get the toughest jobs is because the average Leatherneck is a much better fighter. He has far more guts, courage, and better officers...These boys out here have a pride in the Marine Corps and will fight to the end no matter what the cost"
—2nd Lt. Richard C. Kennard

Chapter Seven

Team Week

THE HOLIDAY SEASON IS A SPECIAL ONE FOR FAMILIES. OUR FAMILY always found a way to meet up and celebrate together, and no matter what kind of disaster it turned into, it was a family disaster.

Now, I was gone.

We were coming together as a platoon and learned to look out for and help each other. So, in one of the most unlikely circumstances I could've envisioned earlier in my life, I had found myself among a new family here.

Then I received a letter from Mom. She had written a special poem for a Marine Christmas and included it.

"On the twelfth day of boot camp, the Marine Corps gave to
*   me . . .*
Twelve weeks of Hell,
Eleven M16 qualifying rounds,
Ten frozen fingers,
Nine chores for team week,
Eight trips to the quarterdeck,
Seven days of swim week,
Six mile humps,
Five minutes of free time,
Four hours of PT,
Three Drill Instructors,

Two sleepless nights,
And one shaved head.

Patrick,

I hope that cheered you up a little bit. Christmas is coming and all we think about is you. Your brother and sister come up a little bit, but they have someone to share the holiday with. So far, for me, it's sucking pretty good, and then I think about you and your shitty conditions. . . How can I complain?

Dad already has a Marine sticker on his car. You can't even shut him up about you and what you've chosen to do. He's proudest father alive.

This anthrax situation is getting really bad, and three Green Berets were killed in Afghanistan. That was a real downer for me. I don't think I could handle it if something happened to you. In fact, I know I couldn't so you just have to stay safe.

Well, I'm signing off for the night. Never forget how much we love you, and you are on our minds always. Merry Christmas, sweetheart.

Love,
Mom"

December 24th, 2001

I have to hand it to my mom for how creative she is. It made me all warm and fuzzy to know how much effort she put in to try and cheer me up.

"Two sleepless nights" and *"eight trips to the quarterdeck"?* I smiled. I could only wish that were the case.

It was team week, which meant one random Drill Instructor, from Mike Company, would show up at night to put us to bed and wake us up in the morning. Most of the platoons were working

92

in the Chow Hall serving food to other recruits. We had been picked for maintenance which meant we would be assigned to random manual labor around the base, but because it was the week of Christmas, the majority were all shut down and there was little to do. We ran on "guide power", meaning our kiss ass little guide called all the shots which set the rest of us to spending most of the day cleaning the squad bay, over and over.

I spent most of the week with Walls and Czarnecki who looked like a little elf and was having problems with his girlfriend of four years, and taking it pretty hard.

"If she ever cheats on me, I swear to God I'll kill her, then myself."

Whoa. He was serious, too. You could see it in his eyes. Walls just rolled his eyes, whistled and walked away.

"You're talking crazy, Czarnecki. It wouldn't be the end of the world," I said to him, trying to bring to some sense of sanity into him. What Rand had said had a lot of validity to it. Especially in their youth, most of the girls back home would move on, if they hadn't already. Czarnecki had been a friend and I didn't want to see him break because the rest of the world kept turning.

"I just love her so much." He had a thick Chicago accent and talked slowly when he was emotional about the subject.

I began to explain to him how life is a string of experiences. I told him about how even situations that seem hopeless end up being funny stories a year or two later. I started giving him examples, from my own life, of relationships, unemployment, and everything else I could think of.

"One time, back at our apartment, Derek and I came home from Wrestle Mania, drunk as hell. Anyway, we're so drunk we just go to our rooms and pass out. A few hours later, I wake up and I'm thirsty from the beer so I go to the kitchen to get a glass of water. The kitchen table's missing and my computer is just sitting on the floor."

93

He started smiling. "What?"

"I was drunk, so I just shrugged and got my water, but when I woke up in the morning I was pissed. My ex-girlfriend came in and robbed us out of over a thousand dollars worth of my stuff... and more importantly, our zoo pictures."

"So, she took the kitchen table, but left the computer?"

I shrugged. "Yeah, she must've needed a kitchen table. You can even take this place, for example. The shit that Rand, McFadden and Kebler have put us through... it's been Hell, but you know one day we're going to wake up in our beds back home. The whole thing is going to seem like a dream, but it's not. It's just going to be a whole bunch of hilarious stories we can tell our friends back home."

He nodded. I think I had actually gotten through to him. "Maybe, you're right."

"No matter how bad something seems, it's always a funny story in the end. As long as I'm breathing, I'm okay."

That night a few of us decided to help the recruits of the other platoons finish up at the Chow Hall. I had been in there for a few minutes when I saw Rand. He parted the sea of recruits in his way like he was Moses... or the devil, and they all leapt out of his way.

I stared. *A few more days, and it's back on.*

He caught my stare and looked back. Like he could read my mind he just looked at me and nodded.

I lay in bed awake that night, alone except for my thoughts, scattered as usual. Derek and Czarnecki were doing rounds on fire watch.

"So, Turley's a pretty good guy, huh?" Czarnecki said as they walked past me in my rack, my eyes closed.

They stopped.

"We've been through a lot together over the years, most of it caused by our own stupidity, and he's always been like this. Unaffected, but caring in his way. I've never seen him waver. A lot of times he didn't know where the next meal would come from, but I'm not sure he ever cared. He's strong. Then we get here and our roles reverse. Well, not reverse, but here we're both like help-less little children and the Drill Instructors our teachers. That was the biggest shock to me. Seeing his eyes burn with anger and for the first time he has to bite his tongue and do what he was told. We're all slaves to circumstance, Czarnecki, but whatever he's talked to you about, and told you, you can trust it."

You always wonder what your friends really think about you. I didn't have that concern and, to this day, couldn't ask for a bet-ter friend than Derek.

I went back to thinking as they continued their fire-watch patrol, about the future, specifically our training in Camp Pendleton and the Crucible, but mostly about the past. It seemed years further and further away every day.

The apartment throbbed with the sound of house music. It was smoky, but most of the smoke had an herbal scent to it.

"You smell that?" I asked Jeremy, smiling.

"Smells like a good night."

It was late. We had come after work and were hours behind everyone else on the youthful race to defile ourselves.

Jeremy cupped a hand over the flame of his lighter as I inhaled until the tip of my cigarette glowed a bright orange. "Thanks," I managed to say from the corner of my mouth with my cigarette still tucked firmly between my lips.

He replied with a curt nod. "So they tried recruiting you into the Marines? Army, maybe, but Marines, that's crazy. I heard people drink bleach there to get out of boot camp."

"Not for me," I said with a slow exhale. "Do you see Theresa anywhere? I don't think I know anyone here."

"Who cares? You should tell me more about that Tammi girl..."

I shrugged as I peered through the smoky haze in the kitchen to the living room. I tapped him on the shoulder and pointed and waved as Theresa looked over in our direction. "There."

She stood up, gesturing for her girlfriends to follow her as she made her way over to us. "Hey, guys. This is Gabrielle and..."

"Angela..." I breathed in disbelief.

"Pat?"

Jeremy's eyebrows perked.

Angela ran over and wrapped her arms around me in a long embrace. "I can't believe it. It's been so long!"

"Okay, what the hell's going on here?" Theresa asked, tugging at Angela's jacket.

I smiled and looked at Theresa. "She's my..."

"Ex," she finished coldly, pushing away from me. "We dated for a little, and then I never heard from him again."

I sighed. "That's not quite what happened." It was though.

"Then what happened?" Theresa asked in her nasally voice.

Jeremy smiled. "I'll tell you what happened. You can't put this animal in a cage."

The girls rolled their eyes and laughed at me in unison.

We settled in and occupied the following hours with small talk, drinking games, and smoking. Jeremy seemed to delight in taking several opportunities to ask about Tammi in front of Angela, who would only reply with pursed lips. The night wore on and eventually, Gabrielle and Angela had to leave.

"Are you going to call me this time?" she asked, putting on her coat.

I cocked my head to the side. "Do you want me to?"

"No," she said, flipping her hair over the collar of her coat as she left.

The next morning we woke up and marched to the Chow Hall. We were standing there for a minute or two when Rand marched thirty-thirty-eight in next to us.

Thirty-eight? We hated thirty-eight, and now, another one of our Drill Instructors was with them... even if only for the morning. I kept staring to the front, until thirty-eight's fourth squad leader leaned down and spit. Some landed on my boot, so I turned around, snorted, and spit a mouthful in his face, igniting the tension. Seconds later and both platoons had turned into an all out brawl.

Rand stood there, folded his arms and watched for a few seconds and then softly said, "Ze-friggin'-ro."

We all froze immediately.

I spent the rest of the day in reflection. I thought mostly about my parents and all the sacrifices they had made for me, and would continue to make. I wasn't sure if I had ever told them how I felt, so I picked up my pen and began to write.

It was the night before Christmas.

Walls had taken the liberty to call the platoon around me so I could read them something.

"Alright, now in my family we have a tradition where every year my father sits down and reads 'The Night Before Christmas', and we all make fun of him as he reads it. Anyway, due to our special circumstances, I wrote our own version for this year." Everyone was gently laughing already. It was an usual feeling adjusting to the holidays in these circumstances. "Alright, here we go:"

> "'Twas the night before Christmas,
> and all through house,
> not a creature was stirring,
> not even recruit Rouse.
> All the M16A2 service rifles,
> were double locked and on safe,
> as we mounted our racks with,

Intensity and Haste.
The recruits lay at the POA,
As Taps eased their fear,
With hopes that Senior Drill Instructor Staff Sergeant
*   Jameson,*
Soon would be here.
Recruit Bruckner stood fire watch,
and recalled the day,
Drill Instructor Staff Sergeant Rand threatened to cave in
*   his kneecap,*
In a unique way.
Out from the head,
arose such a clatter,
as the toilet was stuck,
with our guidon and shattered.
As night wore on,
recruits made head calls often,
but it was still so quiet,
you could 'hear a mouse piss on cotton'.
As morning drew near,
our duties were done,
for fear our Drill Instructors,
would add to our 'fun'.
Revelie came,
and from our racks we flew,
to get on line,
and strip butt naked, too.
The day wore on,
and our expectations grew to finally be surprised with,
nothing."

We all started laughing.

"What the fuck is going on over here?" By luck of the draw
we had gotten McFadden to watch over us tonight.

98

"Nothing, sir!" I yelled. It was nice to have him back again.

"Everyone, get on line, right goddamn now."

We all sprinted on line, and waited for him to finish.

"You should be?"

"Done, sir!" The windows shook harder than they ever had before. Apparently, everyone else was similarly excited to show off the progress we had made to McFadden.

"Hooooooooooooooooooooly shit," he began, his voice drawn out in feigned amazement. "I didn't think it was possible! You all sound even weaker than before. Buncha schoolgirls."

I'll bet.

I had to bite down hard on the inside of my cheeks to stop myself from smiling.

"Just get in the goddamn rack."

"Aye, sir!"

"Shut up!"

"Shut up, aye sir!" we boomed back.

He stormed into the duty hut.

As soon as the lights went out Walls climbed out of his rack and went to his footlocker. "I got a surprise for you, Turley."

"What is it?" I asked with excitement, like I was a little boy again. It was almost Christmas, after all.

Out from his footlocker Walls pulled out four cookies. "The Chaplain gave them to me at Church practice today. I've been hiding them all day. Here take half."

My jaw dropped. I couldn't believe it. I took a bite of one. My mouth exploded in a sensation that it had long since forgotten. "Thank you so much, Walls."

He shrugged, taking a bite himself. "No problem, you've become one of the best friends I've got now," he said in between chews.

"You, too." I said back. *This is the best present I've ever gotten, and I had two of them. Two...*

I got out of bed and slid into my shower shoes and quietly

shuffled to the other end of the squad bay. I shook Derek.

"Hey, wake up buddy."

"Hey, what's up, man?" he asked, looking up at me through squinted, tired eyes.

I held up the cookie and handed it to him. "Merry Christmas, old friend."

His eyes went wide. He didn't ask any questions, just took it and said, "Merry Christmas" back to me.

I went back to my rack and sat down to finish my cookie.

Walls lay in his rack, arms folded behind his head and smiling. "There's a movie at the base theatre for Christmas tomorrow that all the other companies are going to see.."

"Really?"

"Yeah, but I bet the guide won't let us go."

I nodded. "He will if it's an order..."

Walls smiled. "What do you mean?"

I winked through the moonlight. "You'll see tomorrow. Just bring some money to the theatre and buy me some candy and soda."

Walls laughed. "Alright."

It was Christmas day. McFadden had awakened us and then disappeared, as we began to clean the squad bay. Derek came over to me, and we pretended to tighten the linen on my rack as we talked.

Walls said some inane thing to me that I thought was funny.I don't know why I thought it was so funny... maybe it was just the look on his face, combined with the void of humor I had so far experienced, but I started laughing, and then his eyes widened as his face got serious. I turned my head to see McFadden staring at me with his arms folded across his chest.

"Oh, hell-fuck no! We want to be smiling, huh? We're just having a Merry Christmas, aren't we Turley? Well, ho, ho, ho, get on my quarterdeck, right, goddamn, now!"

Fuck.

I stood on the quarterdeck, waiting for some company when Walls hopped out off line and ran over to me.

"What are you doing, Walls?" McFadden called to him.

"This recruit is having a Merry Christmas too, sir!"

"You're a fucking idiot!" Then McFadden stopped in front of Riddle who was standing by his rack.. "Well, well. Riddle me this, Riddle me that, get on my friggin' quarterdeck."

Riddle once told me that when he thought when he said things, he was actually saying them in his head instead of out loud, as if he meant to think it. He said, "Motherfucker," and ran to the quarterdeck.

McFadden just stared in disbelief as he ran by.

So, the three of us stood on the quarterdeck, waiting for punishment. Derek had run back on line, and hid in the back laughing to himself for screwing me over like this. While we waited, I thought of something, and out of the corner of my mouth, whispered it to Riddle and Walls .

McFadden stepped onto the quarterdeck with us and quickly looked us over. "Puuuusssssssh-upppppps!"

"Push-ups, aye, sir!" and we dropped into the push up, position.

When you do Marine Corps push-ups, you drop into the push up position and when given the command "push up" you push yourself up and yell "Marine Corps!" simultaneously.

"Push up!"

"Merry Christmas, sir!" we yelled as we pushed up to the push up position.

I thought the vein pounding wildly in his forehead would pop. "Motherfuckers! You just earned yourself one long, friggin' day! You three are mine. Not even the baby friggin' Jesus can save you, now! I'm gonna..."

And he screamed on and on for at least a half an hour, while we held our push up position, laughing the whole time.

Eventually, McFadden left, and as soon as he did, I was out

the door with Walls. We walked around the recruit depot as fast as we could. I wanted to search for an officer.

"Why are we looking for an officer?" he asked me.

"Just keep your eyes open for the shiny collar." Some services wear shiny chevrons for some pay grades of enlisted ranks. The Marine Corps makes it easy. "If it shines, salute it," and "when it doubt, whip it out."

After only a few minutes we saw one. I smiled to myself, walked up to him and saluted..

"Good morning, sir! Recruit Turley requests permission to speak, sir!" I screamed at the top of my lungs.

He saluted back and looked around for a second, unsure why I would be requesting permission to speak with him

"Okay... what?"

"Recruit Turley requests knowledge, sir!"

He nodded. "Go on."

"Is it the appointed place of duty for these recruits to be at the base theatre for the movie, sir!?"

His forehead crunched up. "Well... it is 'all hands'."

"Aye, sir! Good morning, sir!" I saluted again and waited for him to cut his salute back before turning to walk away.

As we walked away, I turned my head and smiled at Walls. "You understand now?"

He started smiling. "Yup."

I ran up the steps to our squad bay and waved the guide over. "Hey, listen to this. This officer just walks up to us and asks why we aren't marching to the base theatre, because it's 'all hands'. So we say, 'These recruits did not know, sir', and he says, 'Well, hurry up, 'all hands' means 'all hands.' Don't be UA.' So if we don't go, we're UA. I don't think the Senior would like us being UA. 'Don't fuck up', remember?"

UA meant "unauthorized absence" and was taken very seriously.

He nodded, and turned around. "Hey, listen up. Form it up outside. We're going to the movie."

I sat with Walls and Derek and watched "Saving Private Ryan" while I ate, in between sips of Dr Pepper, all the candy I could, all paid for by Recruit Jason Walls.

"Victory is sweet."

After the movie we agreed to never speak of what we had done, marched back, and resumed cleaning.

After an hour or so of day dreaming and looking absently out the window, I casually rubbed with a dry rage, Derek came up to me.

"What's up?" I asked.

He had a serious look on his face. "Derek" and "serious" rarely wound up in the same sentence. I knew something was wrong. He set his hands on the windowsill and we both stared out into space.

"I was looking out the window too, a few minutes ago. Look you can see the homes in the distance with their trees lit up."

Sure enough, outside our barracks, past the fence preventing our escape and past the airport that lay so frustrating close on the other side of the fence, there was a hill with several large houses where you could see the Christmas trees' lights through the windows.

I nodded.

"Well, I just started feeling hopeless, like I would never see another Christmas as long as I live." He paused and looked at me. "My priorities just changed from wanting to be a Marine to getting the easy job during field day..."

I reached up and put my hand on his shoulder. "This will all be over soon, and at least we're going through it together."

Mom and dad,
We leave for Camp Pendleton tomorrow. It's the big unknown

so far, and I'm not sure what to expect. I'm not even sure how often I'll be able to write you, but I can promise, I will as often as possible.

I know that our training is about to become completely different. We're about to start two weeks of the rifle range, and then field week with the gas chamber, and finally finish with the Crucible. I don't really know any details about any of them, but I do know it's not going to be easy.

I'm sorry to hear about dad. I hope work gets better for him. Well, I have to get all my things packed for the bus ride, so have a good day and I love you, and I'll write you as soon as I get the chance.

> *Love,*
> *Patrick"*

"The deadliest weapon in the world is a Marine and his rifle."
—Gen. John "Black Jack" Pershing, U.S. Army
Commander of American Forces in World War I

CHAPTER EIGHT

Up "North"

SOME SAY THAT SUPERIORITY IS REARED IN THE SEVEREST OF SCHOOLS. I used to think I knew everything, now as I learned more and more, the less I felt I really knew. Yet, I did know that I was growing and transforming into the man I was meant to be.

December 30th, 2001

We were all packed up and waiting for the bus. We waited all day for the bus, without really waiting. The Drill Instructors must have missed us because when they came back that day, they gave us even more attention than usual. Most of us were "ITed" three times that day, pushing deck towels and doing push-ups until we were sure our hearts were going to explode.

Rand really missed me. Five times, I got it. *Five times.*

Eventually, the buses came and we got on, nervous about the whole situation. This was the big "unknown" for us. We had adapted and grown as comfortable as we could down here, and yet, now we found ourselves forced to leave it behind to finish our training in Camp Pendleton. We had heard "up north" our officers weren't close by enough to check on us at the squad bays, so the Drill Instructors had free reign to discipline us as they deemed necessary. We only knew our real training began there. The humps, the shooting, the gas chamber, and eventually, the Crucible. The pain was coming and we were all nervous.

Derek and I got on a bus with McFadden, who told us all to, "Shut the fuck up," and went straight to sleep. The bus driver had an easy listening radio station on. It wasn't what I call my "style" of music, but it was quite a pleasant contrast to the incessant barrage of screams to what my ears had become accustomed

McFadden was asleep and in a few minutes, so was I. I passed out and woke up to the sound of an M16 falling and hitting something.

"Who the fuck was that?" McFadden yelled, holding his head.

I looked over. Derek had let go of the rifle in his sleep and it had hit McFadden in the head.

"Bruckner, sir!"

"Brecher, huh?"

Derek looked puzzled. McFadden thought he said "Brecher", another recruit from our platoon.

"Well, I'll make sure Drill Instructor Staff Sergeant Rand hears about this."

"Aye, sir!" Derek yelled back. It was too dark for McFadden to see him smiling and holding back his laughter.

The bus finally arrived at Camp Pendleton, and I stared out the window in curiosity. The sound of "Be My Little Baby" poured from the radio and a sign greeted us: "Armored Vehicles left, Pizza Hut straight".

This is my world, now?

We parked outside our new barracks, much like the one we left down south, and we ran off the bus and McFadden marched us over to our new home.. I was excited.. The rain was pouring down, but I strutted with everything I had as I marched. He halted us and told us to get in the squad bay for our corresponding platoons.

Rand and Kebler were waiting inside and they ran at us, as

soon we broke the threshold, barking orders to get on line. We played musical chairs trying to find our C-bags with all our things, but we didn't move fast enough.

"Mattresses on line!" Kebler yelled.

We ran and grabbed our mattresses as he counted down. They were thicker and heavier than our last ones, but we were all on line, with our mattresses, by the time he hit "three".

"...two, one, you should be?"

"Done, sir!"

"Hold them at the order arms."

Order arms was the rifle manual equivalent to the POA, where you stood, at attention, but rested the muzzle of your rifle on the "v" of your hand between your thumb and forefinger. I wrapped one arm around the back of the mattress and stood at the POA.

"Inspection..."

He can't be serious.

"Arms!"

We all just stood there, looking around and unsure of what to do.

Kebler's nostrils flared. "Okay, fuck me, huh? I know I fucking said, inspection arms."

You've got to be kidding me.

"Inspection... arms!"

We all stood there, trying to wrestle the mattress off of the ground and into our arms.

"Alright, get back! You must all be really trying to piss me off. I didn't see even one of you motherfuckers sandwich it!"

This is absolutely ridiculous.

"Inspection... arms!"

We wrestled them back off the ground and attempted to hoist them up further for steps five and six. I managed to lift mine enough to rest it between my neck and shoulder as I inspected the mattress for its "empty chamber".

And the games went on.

Finally we hit the showers and had our hygiene inspection.

Right before bed, Kebler stepped back out. "Jungle boots in a pile, in the back of the squad bay, right now."

Grudgingly, we all ran with our jungle boots and threw them in a heap on the floor. I sighed to myself before adding to the quickly expanding pile before me. I knew then I would never find the right ones again.

"Just get in the fucking rack, and in the morning all your shit better be neat in your footlockers, your footlockers better be marked and you better have your jungle boots."

No sleep tonight.

I spent the night unpacking my things and marking my footlocker. When morning came I had one size ten left boot and one size eleven and a half right boot. I wore a ten and a half.

Rand woke us up and took us to supply for our "seven-eighty-two" gear, cold weather uniforms, alice packs, sleeping bags and everything else we would need for the field.

Riddle was stooped over digging through all his new equipment. "Polypros, knit beanie, gloves..." He turned and looked at me. "Turley, where's my cold weather jock-strap?"

I laughed back. Whether he was kidding or serious, I don't know. It was borderline impossible to tell with Riddle. Either way, it made my day.

Tomorrow was our first hump and New Year's Eve, and Walls, Derek and I had some special plans.

For the past two months, we had stayed completely bald by having our heads shaved once a week. Now, we were allowed to begin growing the hair on the top of our heads. It was a privilege, a gift that symbolized our progress. It was our transition into third phase. It was time to finish.

We woke up that morning and ate, and then prepared our gear for the hump. A "hump" is the same thing as a hike. It was only three miles, but it was up, over and through the steep hills of Camp Pendleton and with roughly sixty pounds of gear on. Still, it would be over quick.

Soon we moved out and began our first hump. We integrated into two squads, one on each side of the dirt road, and Rand started yelling.

"Listen up, thirty-nine. When I yell, 'heck him', you yell, 'Kill!' and hit the pack of the person in front of you. When I yell, 'AT and T', you yell, 'reach out and touch some body!' and keep your hand on the pack in front of you. When I yell, 'tighter', you yell, 'tighter, aye, sir!' and get tighter. Understood?"

"Aye, sir!"

"Check him!"

"Kill!"

"Check him!"

"Kill!"

It was fun at first, but it continued throughout the entirety of the hump. We were wearing our flak jackets, our Kevlar helmets, our pack full of all our seven-eighty-two gear, and had our rifles slung over one shoulder. We were moving fast. It was bad enough to concentrate on pushing forward up the hills without swinging an arm in front of you to "check him". It was worse when the person behind you used AT&T as an opportunity to cling to your pack and let you drag them.

We kept moving and I noticed we would bunch up for a minute on the hills, and then when we leveled out we would have to sprint to catch up to the platoons in front of us. It was the rhythm the Drill Instructors set for us. Everything was a test. My chest was pounding.

"Tiiiiiiiiiiigh-ter!"

"Tighter, aye, sir!"

"Tiiiiiiiiiiigh-ter!"

"Tighter, aye, sir!" I yelled panting for breath.

"Come here, Mason!" Rand yelled.

Mason broke out of the formation and ran to Rand, panting for breath.

Rand kept his stride and Mason doubled his pace to keep up. Finally, Rand turned his head to look at Mason and said, "Go ask Senior Drill Instructor Staff Sergeant Jameson what time it is."

Mason ran to the front of our formation where Senior Drill Instructor Staff Sergeant Jameson was. "Recruit Mason requests knowledge, sir!"

Senior Drill Instructor Staff Sergeant Jameson gave him a sideways glance. "What is it, Chuck?" He called all of us "Chuck."

"Drill Instructor Staff Sergeant Rand sent this recruit to find out what time it is, sir!" he yelled in between gasps for air.

Jameson looked at him and smiled. "Mason, go tell Drill Instructor Staff Sergeant Rand that he has his own watch."

"Aye, sir! Good afternoon, sir!" Mason yelled and he fell back to Rand.

"Well, what time is it, Mason?"

"This recruit was told that Drill Instructor Staff Sergeant Rand has his own watch, sir!" His breathing was getting even more strained.

Rand almost smiled. "Go tell Senior Drill Instructor Staff Sergeant Jameson that I forgot it," he said back, the face of his watch glistening in the sunlight.

The games went on. I felt sorry for Mason, but in all honesty, I was glad his attention wasn't directed at me this time.

And we pushed on. The time wore on and soon we found ourselves climbing towards a bridge. Kebler slowed down to fall back into the middle of our platoon.

"You all look like shit!" he announced. "Are you trying to embarrass me? Bear-hug the pack in front of you!" he yelled.

Sweat was dripping down my forehead as I fought to push my legs forward, and I grabbed the pack in front of me.

Like every other trial we had undergone so far, it wasn't the hump that was hard, it was all the other bullshit they were putting us through.

But it ended, and as I set my pack down, I began to feel a high. They brought out a Navy Corpsman to check our feet individually down the line and our Senior began talking to us, but all I could think of was our plans for the night.

We had volunteered for fire watch from eleven at night to midnight so we would be awake. As soon as we woke up, we got dressed, and gathered our "supplies".

"A bottle of ibuprofen and three bottles of Listerine?" Derek asked. "Twenty-six percent alcohol," he said, reading the label of the Listerine bottle and nodding his head in approval.

I nodded. "We take ten ibuprofen, slam some Listerine and we'll be drunk for the New Year!"

Walls and Derek started laughing.

"'In case of accidental ingestion, contact Poison Control Center immediately'," I read off the back of the bottle. I shrugged. "The keyword is accidental... it doesn't say a goddamn thing about intentional ingestion." I raised a bottle of Listerine. "Drink with me to days gone by."

Derek raised his. "Sing with me the songs we knew."

"Happy New Year, guys."

"Happy New Year," Derek said back.

"Happy New Year," echoed Walls. "My New Year's resolution is to never join the Marine Corps again."

We laughed... and we drank.

Bang, bang, bang. "The time on deck is zero-five-thirty, sir!"

Every morning began that way, but often you were so exhausted you slept until the calls of "Lights! Lights! Lights!" At a designated time the morning fire-watch would bang on the hatch of the duty hut and announce the time on deck at fifteen minute intervals or as directed by the Drill Instructor on duty. New Year's Day it went on, and on, and on, and on...

Come zero-seven-hundred we were all already awake, head-calls had been made and the morning had become more awkwardly ominous than anything. I quietly shuffled over to the fire-watch at the quarterdeck, a big southern boy named Bailor. "What's going on?" I asked.

Bailor shrugged with a defeated look painted across blocky features. "He told us to shut the fuck up..."

Eventually, Rand exploded from the duty hut and started dispensing the wrath we all knew was coming. He looked hung over, and frankly, I didn't feel too fresh either.

Naturally, everything was blamed on Bailor as we were raced to get ready and off to the chow hall, already late for our tightly scheduled day. "When we get back to the house... oh, when we get back to the house, you're all gonna pay," he promised, over and over as we marched.

Once we had returned to the house and gotten online, Drill Instructor Staff Sergeant Rand stood firmly before us, looking every bit the cold blooded predator. "You've all been cleared by the Senior Drill Instructor to watch a movie today." Immediately our hopes went high. "He thinks you deserve it. I don't. And guess who's fucking here?" You could feel hope and the last vestiges of optimism deflate from the squad-bay. If nothing else, the man keeps his promises. "So we're going to do what I think you deserve. Get in the mud outside and start low crawling, right now."

And so we played games, all day. We could hear movies like "Pearl Harbor" and "Braveheart" coming from the squad bays of our rival platoons adding to our frustration, and there we were, crawling back and forth in the fresh mud from the new year's first drops of rain.

Happy New Year. I could almost hear the sound of kazoos going off in my head as I thought it.

"Get on line, right now!"

We ran in, mud falling from our boots and cammies all over the house, and fell in on line at the POA.

Rand walked up to me, and slowly inhaled. "You don't look good today, Turley. Are you feeling okay?"

"Yes, sir!"

Rand walked into the duty hut only to emerge with an ax in hand.

"Open your footlocker."

"Aye, sir!" I said and dropped to my haunches, racing to open my combination lock.

"Could you move any slower?"

"Yes, sir!" I said. I heard a loud thud as the ax head landed into my footlocker. My eyes went wide as I stared at the blade only a few inches from my face.

"Too slow." Rand wrenched my footlocker open, and pulled out a half-empty bottle of Listerine. "Well, well... have you and Walls been getting drunk in the gear locker?" he asked while unscrewing the cap.

"No, sir!"

He began to pour the rest of the bottle out on my face. "You look sick today... I think we should hydrate, so you feel better, Turley." He turned and faced the rest of the platoon. " Canteens out, right now!"

In this particular game, we would chug both our canteens of water, and pause only long enough to refill them, Rand always checked to make sure they were full, and we had learned months ago that the penalties of trying to sneak a half filled canteen far outweighed the potential reward, and we would begin the cycle again. After about six canteens, your stomach starts to turn. When you try to force more water in you throw up a forceful jet stream of water. Oddly enough, during this release your stomach doesn't wrench, your throat doesn't burn, it doesn't even leave a bad taste in your mouth, it only leaves you dizzy... it's almost fun, but now we had mud and chunks of vomit all over the floor.

"You've got thirty seconds to clean my goddamn floor... thirty, twenty-nine, twenty-eight..."

It was our square away time.

I stood outside at the trough with Walls, trying as best we could to clean our sweat soaked and filthy cammies. Derek stood across the way doing the same.

He looked across at us and asked if we'd like to join him in his canoe, before pantomiming canoeing across the trough. He followed it up with stairs, the elevator and escalator.

I was nearly doubled over in laughter when I stopped and my face must have gone white. Derek's eyes went wide immediately when he realized what the sudden change meant.

He glanced behind to find Drill Instructor Staff Sergeant Rand, watching through the barracks window, arms folded and stone face seething in rage.

This night was not going to end well.

We snapped in the next week. Snapping in was getting your body used to the positions we would be shooting from in the following week, and learning the skills we needed to kill a man from five hundred yards. It was during this week we would start to piece together the deliberate methodology of the inane details of the past two months. Everything had been left over from bootlaces to our sitting position. We would shoot left leg over right. When we "took a knee", we had been doing it in the kneeling position to shoot. We had been conditioning our bodies to be completely still for hours on end. The reality was that we had been "snapping in" from the moment we stepped foot onto the Marine Corps Recruit Depot.

Our Drill Instructors handed out our "data books" which we

would be using to record our shooting. I opened the first page and began to read:

"This is my rifle. There are many like it, but this one is mine.

My rifle is my best friend. It is my life. I must master it as I must master my life.

My rifle, without me, is useless. Without my rifle, I am useless. I must fire my rifle true. I must shoot straighter than my enemy who is trying to kill me. I must shoot him before he shoots me. I will...

My rifle and myself know that what counts in this war is not the rounds we fire, the noise of our burst, nor the smoke we make. We know that it is the hits that count. We will hit...

My rifle is human, even as I, because it is my life. Thus, I will learn it as a brother. I will learn its weaknesses, its strength, its parts, its accessories, its sights and its barrel. I will ever guard it against the ravages of weather and damage as I will ever guard my legs, my arms, my eyes and my heart against damage. I will keep my rifle clean and ready. We will become part of each other. We will...

Before God, I swear this creed. My rifle and myself are the defenders of my country. We are the masters of our enemy. We are the saviors of my life!

So be it, until victory is America's and there is no enemy, but peace!"

"Good morning."

"Good morning, sir!"

He started smiling. "My name is PMI Sergeant Casanova. PMI stands for 'primary marksmanship instructor'. This week is going to be a little different for you. I'm not going to be a dick, because learning to shoot is very important in the Marine Corps, and I think you need a fun learning environment. Alright, who knows some jokes?"

Derek looked over at me and I nodded back, so he stood up first and told our favorite joke. "Bacon, eggs, and ham walk into a bar. The bartender looks at them and says, 'Sorry, guys, we don't serve breakfast.'"

I'm not sure what it is but I crack up every time I hear, or tell that joke.

No one else laughed except Walls and I.

"Okay.... anyone else?"

"This recruit, sir!" His name was Wilson. He was a funny kid, and one of the few I was actually thankful for being in our platoon.

"Go ahead."

"These three midgets are sitting around watching TV when they see a show about the Guinness Book of World Records. So one midget says, 'I've got some real tiny feet, I'll bet I have the smallest feet in the world!' The next midget says, 'Hey, look at my hands, I'm sure I'll win the world's smallest hands!' The last midget says, 'I'll bet I have the smallest dick in the world! You can barely see it!'

"So the midgets head down to the Guinness World Records place to get measured and the first one goes in. Ten minutes later the first midget comes out all happy and says, 'I'm in! I'm in! I have the smallest feet in the world!' So then the second midget goes in, and he comes out a half an hour later all excited, 'I did it! I have the world's smallest hands!' So the third midget is feeling all confident about having the world's smallest penis as he walks in. After an hour and a half the third midget walks out all depressed, so the other midgets ask what happened and he says, 'Who the fuck is PMI Sergeant Casanova?'"

We all stood there in the bleachers stunned. We were trying to fight the laughter, but it was really too funny to hold back. I

116

couldn't believe he had the balls to tell a joke like that and use our PMI as the punch line. If Rand had found out one of his recruits had used a Marine as a punch line, Wilson would have signed his own death warrant. Sergeant Casanova stood for a minute shaking his head before he started laughing himself.

The rest of the week was the same. We woke up and ate, every meal was egg noodles and a head of lettuce for salad, then we would met PMI Casanova at the "snap in circles" and have our class. We learned how to adjust for windage, and how to find correct sight alignment and correct sight picture, the elements we would need to effectively kill through iron sights. Then we would go over our sitting, kneeling, standing, and prone positions and aim in on a barrel.

I was growing attached to Angel, significantly more than if I had the actual woman behind it. Every time I read "My Rifle" it got worse.

On Friday, we shot for the first time. We had three rounds to shoot at a paper target so we could find our grouping and adjust for our "true zero". Everyone shoots a rifle differently, so you need to find your grouping and adjust it up and to the right or down and to the left, until your grouping is in the target itself... that's your true zero.

I felt a rush of power wash over me with those three rounds. The M16 barely recoiled as I squeezed the trigger, intent on killing my imaginary foe. My eyes grew wide as I shot and my breathing turned heavy. It was addictive and it was over far too fast.

All the next week we would be shooting, but first, we had the five mile beach hump to get through the next day,.

It began just like the last hump had. Tighter and AT&T and any other ways they could find to keep us short of breath and battling through frustration. After a mile or two we hit the beach and then everything went to hell.

My boots would sink an inch or two into the sand, and my

heels would twist as I tried to step out, yet the pace quickened instead of slowing, and we all fought to stay in formation.

Recruits began falling out everywhere. I ran through the sand yelling, "Tighter, aye, sir!" as I went. Waves of self-doubt and despair began to wash over me. I could hear recruits in front, behind and to the right screaming. I took my frustration out by yelling back, as hard as I could, when they yelled, "tighter", or "check him".

I was beginning to have serious doubts if I would finish, and started to think about how easy it would be to just fall out and ride through the rest of this torture in a truck, like many already had. Immediately after, I hated myself for even thinking it. That wasn't me. I was here for a reason, and I would earn it the right way, or not at all, and I pushed on.

I laughed away the frustration.

Let the weak ones fall. I am stronger.

And then it was over...

It was a dark, sleazy bar. Dim, smoky, and the inhabitants far from classy. They ranged from alcoholics to biker gangs. For Derek and I, it was a second home. We had streaks where we would drink there every night for weeks, taunting fate by angering the clientele with an endless barrage of "Who Let the Dogs Out?" on the jukebox or through our usual carefree, obnoxious behavior. When I first opened the door, I choked and coughed on the smoke and I was a smoker.

There's no place like home, I thought to myself.

"Hey, Derek, Pat's here." It was Andy, our bartender who gained two loyal customers by never thinking of asking for our identification. He always took good care of us. Over the past year we'd gotten to know each other well, and besides, Derek and I were good tippers.

"Well hurry up, Sally, you're a pitcher behind," Derek yelled to me as I sat down on the stool next to him.

Wordlessly, Andy set a pitcher of High Life down in front of me with a frosted glass beside it.

"How was work?" I asked Derek, pouring myself a beer from my pitcher.

"The same." He shrugged. "Nothing really happens in Elm Grove."

I laughed back. He was right. What could there possibly be for police to do in a small, upper-class village in Wisconsin outside of harassing high school kids and handing out tickets for rolling stops?

"I'm gonna play some music. Anything you want to hear?"

"You know what I want."

I nodded my response as I collected my beer and a cigarette to make the one yard trek to the jukebox. We generally either played "Wang Dang Sweet Poontang" by Ted Nugent-where we could swear the only lyrics were "Well wang dang for the sweet poontang!"— or something woefully out of character for the bar, because the absurdity made us laugh. I smiled as he made my selection and headed back to the barstool.

Derek rolled his eyes as he tried to avoid an older man to his left, reeking of booze. "So what's new with you?"

I nodded my head as I took another drink. "Remember that Angela girl?"

Derek laughed for a moment. "How do you expect me to remember? I stopped caring months ago," he said through tight lips as he lit his cigarette.

"Come on." I slapped the counter top. "Angela from like, seven months ago."

The old man nudged Derek with his elbow then. "Where were ya born, kid?"

I fought back my smile and gave Derek a questioning look.

He turned his head. "Poontang, Wisconsin."

Derek, no.

He looked back at me. "The one you stopped calling, right?"

119

"Yes!"

The older man nudged Derek again. Through extremely slurred speech, he said, "I always thought that was a... well you know... slang word for a woman's... ya know?"

Derek looked back at him, gently shaking his head, and somehow maintaining a straight face. "No, I don't know." He looked back at me. "I still don't remember this girl."

"Then how did you know?"

"Because that's what you do."

"Vagina!" the older man exclaimed with an all too intense look on his face.

I couldn't hold back the laughter this time.

Derek turned back to face him. "Look. I don't know what brought this on, but I don't need to sit here and listen to obscenities! Poontang, Wisconsin. It's near Eau Claire." The drunk shrank back into his chair, feeling scolded. I only laughed harder. "So what about this girl?"

"Anyway, I ran into her the other day while you were working."

"...and?"

I shrugged.

Derek nodded. "What about Tammi?"

I just drank.

"So what I'm taking away from this is that you're wasting your time talking, so you're still a pitcher behind."

I laughed again and finished my beer. "You're right... priorities. Beer first. It won't happen again," I swore, holding a hand to my heart. I poured myself another from the pitcher.

I hid my face in my hands while I started to laugh as "Can you feel the love tonight" started to play over the jukebox. It only took a second to recover and then we both joined the angry crowd of the bar in feigned outrage and yelled vague threats to find whoever played it, until the anger died down.

Derek sighed after taking another long drink. "I tell ya, man. Elton John can soothe my soul any day…"

I paused, unsure of what I'd heard. "...excuse me?"

"What?"

"What did you say?"

"I said, 'Elton John can soothe my soul any day'."

I gave him the kind of vacant stare that you could usually only see from Bert on Sesame Street. After several long moments that weren't nearly as awkward as they should have been, I said, "You know that Elton John is gay, right?"

He cocked his head to the side. "What?"

"Elton John, he's gay."

Derek just sat there in stunned disbelief. Eventually his shocked expression turned into one of revelation. "Well I guess that explains the hats."

"And 'Don't let the son of a bitch go down on me'."

We laughed and refocused on our business of drinking ourselves silly when suddenly Derek stopped and turned. "Wait a second. Is this the girl we tried to find at Parkbar?"

I nodded.

"Why didn't you say so? What are you going to do?"

I shook my head. "What I do best. Nothing."

He laughed into his drink before looking back at the pool table and nodding back at me. "Want to play pool?"

"War paint?" I asked.

"War paint," he affirmed, smiling back.

It was Sunday before the rifle range, and Derek and I were sitting next to each other at Church.

"Guess what I was thinking about last night?" I asked Derek.

"Beer, money, women, sex?"

"No. Remember when we used to play pool at Speedway and take the cue chalk and draw blue war paint all over our faces?"

Derek shook his head at me and let himself laugh. "Maybe you should get out a little more."

I laughed back.

121

"Walls, when this is over, if it ever ends, we go drinking, and whoever shoots worse pays. Sound good?"

He nodded and smiled. "Alright."

I walked to my target with Angel and sat on the ready bench. It was my turn to shoot next. I put my ear plugs in. It felt almost like swim week. The sound around me was swept away immediately and I felt at peace. Angel was sitting on my knee, muzzle up perpendicular to the ground. I didn't even notice I was softly stroking her.

I was focused and determined to connect with every round. I had memorized "My Rifle" and I began to slowly recite it under my breath as I stroked Angel up and down.

"This is my rifle.." I said to myself as I walked up to the firing line.

"With the magazine of five rounds, Load!" came booming from the sound shed off to my far left.

I pulled out my magazine and slammed it home.

"There are many like it, but this one is mine."

"Shooters on the firing line, make ready!"

I jerked back on the charging handle, checked to make sure the round chambered, and pressed the forward assist.

"My rifle is my best friend."

"Is the firing line ready? Ready on the left, ready on the center, ready on the right. Shooters you may commence firing when your targets appear... targets!"

"It is my life." I said while I fought for correct sight alignment and correct sight picture. I breathed deep.

I exhaled. "I must master it as I must master my life..." and fired.

Bull's-eye after bull's-eye.

"Turley, come here!"

The Senior was calling me over. I was proud. After all, I was sure he wanted to congratulate me on how good I was shooting on the first day. What else? The series commander and the chaplain were waiting there with him. I ran up and stood at port arms and yelled, "Good morning, gentlemen."

Captain Wiles grabbed the M16 out of my hands. "Let me see it, Killer," he said to me, not even giving me a chance to run a proper inspection arms before handing it off.

I was confused now.

Senior Drill Instructor Staff Sergeant Jameson looked at me. His face was stone cold. "I've got some bad news, Chuck." Right then and there I knew what he was about to say. "It's your dad, he's dead."

The chaplain took me off the range and talked to me for a minute, but I didn't know what to say, or if any of this was actually real. They were sending me home, and I had the option to stay there, to not come back. The chaplain told me most people in my situation don't come back, and it would probably be a good idea to stay home and get my emotions in line.

"You could come back and try again when you're ready," he offered, his voice laden with compassion.

Try again? I hadn't failed anything. I had poured my everything into this place. *Am I dreaming?*

An hour later I went back to the range. I was supposed to find Drill Instructor Staff Sergeant Kebler, and he was going to handle it from there. Some of the other Drill Instructors from the series found me first. They tied my hands behind my back with duct tape and began pushing me around, yelling that I was "nasty" and that "the Marine Corps didn't want me, anyway" and spitting in my face. For once, there was no rage sweeping through my body. Only shock. I just stood up and let them do what they wanted. I was too wounded from the day for them to be able to affect me. I had spent my life feeling a mixture of being untouchable and invincible, only to discover how fragile I truly am beneath my resilience. Then Rand came in and pushed them all back away from me.

One of the Drill Instructors from thirty-thirty-seven gave him a dirty look and said, "What are you mad at me for? I didn't kill his dad."

Rand pulled the tape off my hands and turned me around until we stood eye to eye, like we had so many times before. "You okay?" he asked in his normal voice.

He had a normal voice?

I didn't say anything. I just stood there staring off into space until Kebler showed up. I could hear Derek behind me yelling, "Recruit Bruckner requests permission to speak to recruit Turley!" over and over again as loud as he could, as I followed Kebler off to the airport.

"Courage is endurance for one moment more..."
—Unknown Marine Second Lieutenant in Vietnam

CHAPTER NINE

Homecoming

I HAD SPENT NIGHT AFTER NIGHT WONDERING, TO MYSELF, HOW IT would feel being in the real world again How would I react to the freedom of my place in Wisconsin or with my folks in Arizona? Or would I think it was all a bad dream and everything would be back to normal? Now I knew, and all I could do was lay there and wish it was a dream... wish I were still in Hell. My wishes were never answered.

January 9th, 2002

The night before, I had made my return home. I had dreamed of my homecoming to my folks in Arizona. I dreamed of how badly I wanted to see everyone's faces, smiling and proud. Now they were empty and tear-stained. This was the moment I had dreamed of, but not like this.. My mother ran to me, through the airport, like nothing else existed in the world. I grabbed her in my arms as she lay her head on my shoulder and cried as hard as she could. My brother and sister weren't far behind. I tried to smile, but I couldn't, so I quietly walked to the car.

"Are you hungry?" my mother asked, turning her head slightly to look at me while driving. Mascara still streaked her cheeks.

Was I hungry? I hadn't even noticed that I had barely eaten today, or for the past two months for that matter. "Very."

We stopped for Mexican so I could begin eating chips and salsa immediately. There was an eerie feeling among us. No one knew what to say or what to do. So, we sat there, silently, and ate.

The food came and within moments, I was done, plate clean.

My mother gave me an odd look. "You don't like guacamole or tomatoes."

I looked down at my place. *Clean.* "I guess I do."

We made it home and my mother disappeared for a moment, giving me time to find my whiskey and fix myself a drink. I took a long drink and noticed I was staring at the laundry room. The glass almost fell from my hands.

The laundry room was where I should have been. Where I could have caught him when he fell, and called an ambulance, where I could have saved my father's life.

My mother came back up behind me and rubbed my back with one hand. "I know, honey," she told me.

For me, there were no words.

She had a letter in her hands, it was something I wrote, and began to read it to all of us.

Dad,

You wrote in your last letter that you thought you'd make a 'crappy Marine'. I've never heard anything further from the truth. Since I've gotten here, I've learned being a Marine isn't about action, being in shape, and looking good in a uniform. I've learned it's about honor and integrity and standing for what is right. The only reason I know anything about integrity and honor, is what I know from you. These qualities represent everything you are.

I know you weren't always around when I was little. You were off, for work, doing everything you could to provide for our family, and I never thought of it as not caring. We always understood. And when you were gone, you did everything you

126

*could to make it back for important things like our birthdays
and Christmas.*

*We never really talked much, like some fathers and sons do,
but that was because of me, and I always knew that if I ever
needed to, you would drop everything just to listen. Some days
it may not seem like it, but we all love you with everything we've
got and we appreciate everything you've done for us. I love you,
Dad. Hope everything back home is going great.*

Love,

Patrick

PS. Don't get the wrong idea, you're still a shitty driver."

Everyone laughed at the last part and then began to thank me
for saying what they felt on their behalf. Everyone was looking
at me and waiting for me to say something to reassure them. I
had to more than ever.

I forced myself to smile. "One night, at about two a.m., Derek
went to the bathroom, it's the only time we have a chance to go,
and he sprawls out on the toilet. Well, one of my Drill Instructors
happened to come through the bathroom and sees him, and, of
course starts screaming, 'What position do we shit at Bruckner?'
So, Derek snaps up on the toilet and yells, 'POA, sir!'"

They laughed.

I began telling more stories and eventually jarred my brother's memory, a former Marine himself, to where he began telling
some of his own. It was helping.

The laughing ended and my mood changed. I could no longer
be reassuring.. I could no longer smile. I stood up and retired to
my room, whiskey in hand.

I took my Charlie's off as fast as I could. Two months ago, it
would have been another set of clothes to me. Now, I didn't feel
that I deserved to wear that uniform. Yet. My brother claimed
that the Marine Corps killed creativity, my friend Mike that it

127

"brainwashed." Maybe Mike was right.

I took another drink and unfolded the letter my brother had handed to me, earlier in the day.

"Patrick,

Hi, right now I'm not sure what to say. Mom's sitting next to me and she wants to write you, so badly, but she's so drained and overcome that she can't bring herself to, right now. My mind's going a thousand different ways, right now. Mom and I feel terrible that you had to find out from someone outside the family. It's not right. We both wish you weren't in boot camp, right now. It's not fair for you to find out and deal with it there. It's not fair that Mom's without a husband. It's not fair Dad lost his life at only fifty-five years old. They say, 'when it's your time to go, it's your time to go. Bullshit! It wasn't his time to go. He had your graduation, my wedding, and a grandchild to see, plus retirement. Not one day of retirement will he and mom spend together. I don't know what else to say or even do with myself next. I hope to God they let you come home for the funeral. I love you, Pat.

Randy"

Why? Was I dreaming or was this all real? Words echoed in my head, pounding at the walls of my mind, *"Relax, Dad, it's not like it's the last time we'll see each other."*

I stood there in the parking lot with Derek and my Dad.

It was dark now and we had to get going. It was time for goodbye. I wouldn't see my father for three months. It was no big deal, we'd gone for longer than that a half-dozen times.

"Alright, Dad, I'll see you in three months," I said as I hugged him hard.

He hugged back harder... harder than I'd ever felt before. "I'm so proud of you," he said, voice twisting as tears welled up in his eyes.

I was confused. He wasn't the stoic and cold father figure many had, but I had never really seen him get this emotional before. "Relax, Dad," I told him. "It's not like it's the last time we'll see each other."

I should have said something else. I should have stayed with him. Fuck, I could have caught him. *I should have...*

...and morning came.

So there I was, lying in bed with one hand fumbling for the whiskey bottle. My mind raced through memories I couldn't shut out, no matter how hard I tried. I couldn't help but feel, that at age twenty, my better days were already behind me.

I had been given the same speech, repeatedly, about "God's will", "He works in mysterious ways", and "Having other plans for him." The same generic bullshit everyone is fed when they have been forsaken by such a "kind" and "merciful" God.

The finality of my situation was nearly impossible to grasp. It seemed like he was just on another business trip, and would come home any day now. But, that was not the case. I wanted answers, but knew I would get none.

"Relax, Dad, it's not like it's the same time we'll see each other."

Why was I such an idiot?

For the first time in two months, I walked away from my bed, unmade. It didn't feel right. I walked into the kitchen, wearing only my boxers. Greg was there. He was an ex-Navy pilot from Vietnam and had flown for the Blue Angels. He was my father's best friend. They had shared experiences, from work, throughout the world. Now, he was walking my mother through the funeral preparations for Friday.

"Oh, Patrick, you're up," Greg said, noticing my entrance into the room, "and dealing with everything well, I see." The last part was directed towards my hand which still held my whiskey.

I answered by raising my eyebrows and taking another drink. I stretched my neck from side to side and set Mr. Jack Daniels on the counter. It was time for a new bottle, after all.

"How's boot camp treatin' ya? Like crawling around with a knife in your mouth?"

I couldn't really recall ever crawling around with a knife in my mouth, but the simplest answer was the simplest way out. "Can't get enough."

He had brought pastries stuffed with different fruits over for breakfast. There were five left, and none when I was through.

Under different circumstances, this would have been paradise. Here I was, drinking heavily, eating as much as I could, sleeping late, and being "nasty" in general. I didn't notice, however. My mind was elsewhere, and at this point I wasn't sure if it would ever come back.

Was this all there was to life? A constant stream of painful experiences to shake you to your core and test your resolution? I thought of Czarnecki and the conversations we shared... the advice I gave, about every experience in life ending up being another funny story in the end, no matter how painful it seems at the time. Yeah, that was me. Everything was funny to me. I wasn't laughing now. I couldn't fathom how this could ever be another "funny story."

Life had always been a game to me. Billions of people in a mad rush to get their hands on all they could before they die. Just a game, but, it was a game I didn't want to play anymore.

That night, my brother asked me to join him by the fireplace outside the house for some drinks so we could talk.

It was a beautiful scene.

The outside lights danced across the surface of our pool. It was a clear, smooth emerald surface. Perfect and undisturbed until the waterfall started up, cascading down the rocks and into the water with a nearly inaudible splash, sending gentle ripples across the pool to the tile edges. Water always calmed me. It always took the pain away, but not now. Now, I found my eyes were more eagerly attracted to the fire my brother had started. The flames flickered violently, echoing the anger burning within me... within my soul.

I snapped out of my reverie as we began to talk. We talked about boot camp, life, death, and religion. We talked about his fiancée and, of course, my inability to maintain interest in a woman longer than six months. He explained to me that it was because I only dated supermodel types with no substance. It was flattering at first, until I realized he was right and felt petty.

"It's amazing you wrote that letter, when you did, Pat. Thank you so much."

I found myself drawn back to the flames. "I, I think I knew," I said slowly, trying to tear the words out from my mouth.

He just nodded.

We started talking again about my father, and all he had accomplished. Everything from his roots of hunting rabbits simply to be able to eat, to African business trips in war-torn, mercenary laden countries, and having to be evacuated by the CIA. Mainly, though, we talked about everything he stood for. He was the most honest man anyone would ever meet, and a genius who could do any task he set his mind to. His work had always taken advantage of that, but the needs of our family always came first. His was a legacy that neither of us had any chance of repeating.

My brother looked up at me. "You're the one, you know that right?"

My father had believed in me above all else. He was convinced if I tried I could do anything shy of walking on water. Until that

131

point, however, I had never realized how much my brother believed in me.

This time, it was I who could only nod.

"So, back together again?" Derek said laughing.

"Yeah, pretty much."

"Definitely going to work out this time," Derek said, voice dripping sarcasm through continued laughter as he grabbed two beers from the refrigerator. He handed one to me as he sat down on the couch at my side. I twisted the cap off and took a drink before turning on the news.

"September Tenth?" I shook my head. "September Tenth. For Christ's sake... where has the time gone? Where are we going to end up? I won't be bartending forever. What about you? What are you thinking?"

"I'm getting paid to nap by the dispatch phones at the police department... *and* I haven't gotten a ticket since I started." He took a drink. "About the future, though, we'll figure that out tomorrow."

I nodded and turned my attention back to the television.

Tomorrow... he meant it metaphorically... the future and tomorrow. But he would be right. Tomorrow, in fact, we would figure out our future.

I stared at the weatherman giving the usual Wisconsin forecast of "snow, snow and more snow.". "I wonder what he thinks."

"He thinks you think too much."

"He's probably right," I admitted. "You working tonight?"

"Yeah," he replied standing up and taking another drink. "Give me a call and wake me up if you want." He finished his beer and set it down on the coffee table. "Well, I'm off to the police department."

I spent most of the night drinking with the radio playing in the background and trying to assemble some random thoughts on my computer, musing to myself over potential stories I could write. I had grown so accustomed to late nights at the bar, that before I knew it, the sun was rising. I rubbed at my eyes realizing I had nearly fallen asleep, the radio now broadcasting a "shock jock" based out of Chicago. I brushed my teeth and made my way to bed and had nearly drifted into unconsciousness when Mancow the radio guy claimed a plane had crashed into one of the Twin Towers.

That's not funny, I thought. It had to be a joke.

I pushed myself out of bed and turned the television back on.

My eyes lit up in horror and my mind instantly grew sober. *It's true.* I lit a cigarette, unable to tear my eyes away from the screen. The image staring back at me was of the first tower, billowing smoke. At first, I thought some idiot in a private prop plane had gotten lost, and the whole thing just a terrible accident. Then the second plane hit. It felt like the end of the world.

I picked up the phone.

"Hey, what's up buddy? Just woke up..."

"Turn on the news, Derek."

"What?"

"Just do it."

"Okay... what's going on?v

"I'll call you back later."

"Alri..."

I hung up.

I dug through one of the kitchen draws where we kept randomly discarded items. I sat back on the couch rolling the business card around in my fingers with one hand, holding a never ending chain of cigarettes in the other, and watched as the two towers fell to the ground.

I looked down at the card. Maybe it wasn't the end of the world, but it was the end of mine.

133

We had awakened that morning and decided to head to Squaw Peak, a suburban Arizona, steep hiking trail that my mother and I had climbed before. We got out of the car and, after a few quick stretches, began our ascension.

Shortly after we started, my mind went blank. To this day, I'm not clear on what had happened, but my mind had entered into some sort of void. I started running, no, sprinting as hard as I could, leaving my mother and brother behind, dodging other hikers, leaping from rock to rock over mile long sheer drops, and making my own path as I saw fit. I had never been so focused in my life, and within minutes, I had reached the summit.

I stood there in a daze, not quite sure how I had gotten there, my chest heaving and begging for air. There was a tiny American flag that marked the peak. That damn thing had gotten me into this whole mess. I walked up beside it and, with my back turned to the city view of Phoenix, took a seat to stare out into the mountain range.

The drop off was steep. The valley below had a few trees and bushes, offsetting the earth tones of the rest of the desert landscape. My mind started wandering again, the focus lost. If your body is only a shell, where does what lies within go when that shell is broken? Logically, it made sense that it would spread back out over the Earth, like a glass of water on the table. When the glass gets broken the water spreads out along the surface. So, maybe my dad was here, all around me. It was comforting.

"Hey, up there."

There goes comfort. I wasn't happy to be interrupted. I looked down.

She was tanned and pretty, and climbing up towards me, with tiny shorts and a sports bra framing a perfect body, from what I saw. "I've never seen anyone run this that fast. I'm Ericka" she said extending her little hand and cocking her hips. She seemed interested.

I wasn't. "I'm sorry," was all that I said back, returning my stare to the valley before me.

Out of the corner of my eye, I saw her go wide-eyed and let her jaw drop a bit as she turned to walk away. She wasn't used to that kind of treatment, I was sure. Any other time and my response would have been significantly different, but this was not any other time. I only wanted some time alone with my thoughts as I tried to regain that comfort.

It was some time later that my mother and brother caught up, panting for breath. I got up and ran over and then further past them. "Let's go," I said with a deep exhale, bouncing back down the trail.

That night, I found myself out by the fire, again, with my brother and Tom.

Tom was our builder. a young multimillionaire who had become close friends with my mother and father during the building of our house, and the man who had found my father dead on the tile floor of the laundry room. He came over to speak with my mother and visit with us all, but before long he had drinks of his own outside by the fire.

We talked a long time, that night. We talked about our lives and the future. We shared more stories about my father. Tom began to tell us about how "Barry" had brought Christmas presents over for his daughters in the middle of the night, so they wouldn't find them until Christmas morning. Sometimes, just a small gesture can mean everything, and to his family, it did.

It was cold outside. When night fell on the desert, the relative temperature cut right to the bone. Tom suggested we jump in the pool "for Barry." I couldn't possibly understand the connection between my father and hypothermia, but these days I was having trouble deciding up from down, so who was I to judge?

I was the first one down to my boxers and into the pool.

When everyone left, I went to check on my mother. She was

crying alone in her room, again. I opened the door and walked in and held her while she cried. It was another time where no words could be found. After all, the viewing was tomorrow.

I had never been truly afraid of anything. Yet, here I was forcing myself to breathe as I stared down at the door handle before me. My heart pounded harder than I had ever felt it. My blood turned to lava coursing through my veins. I knew what was on the other side of that door. When that handle turned, I would be face to face, again, with my father. Only this time, he was dead in a box.

I wasn't ready. I would never be ready. How could this have happened? Thoughts began to pour into my head, setting my mind racing, again. I couldn't make it stop. *Please God make it stop*, I thought to myself. With a deep breath, I reached out for the door handle and twisted.

My sister went in first and with a cry of "Oh my God," burst into an uncontrollable sob. My brother and mother followed with similar reactions. I tried to steel myself, and followed.

Time froze. There he was, eyes closed in a box with a green blanket covering him up to the chest. My mother wasn't sure where she would end up in life, so she made the decision to have him cremated, so eventually, they could be buried together. Due to the impending cremation, the funeral had opted not to use any make-up on him. His face was purple with a huge black bruise from forehead to cheek where his face had smacked into the tile floor. A face always so filled with happiness and love, now empty and lifeless.

For the past few years, I had become emotionless, never letting my own feelings touch me or cloud my thinking. As I crossed the room, in what seemed like slow motion, with my family sobbing violently behind me at the vision of my dead father, the dam broke. I found myself in the corner, sunken down to my knees, and for the first time in years, tears streamed uninhibited down my face. It wasn't the sight of my father or anything about the environment that brought on my hysteria. It was reality. It was knowing, now, he was gone. It was accepting that life, as I knew it, was over... forever.

If I had thought my blood boiled before, it seared now. My rage at the world welled up inside me, the flames within built upon themselves until an inferno raged inside, forcing me into submission and making me surrender. All I could do was cry, and then it was over.

We managed to regain composure, eventually. We hugged each other and talked about how the family would have to stay strong. My brother even tugged on one of my father's disgusting toes protruding from the blanket and joked, "Yeah, that's Dad, alright." As everyone turned to leave, I asked to stay behind for another minute.

The room empty now, just me and the shell of my hero. The room, and the world all around it, felt lifeless and cold.

I grabbed one of my father's cold, limp hands and kneeled down next to him. "Dad, life isn't worth living without you," I began, tears welling back up to resume their path down my cheeks. "But I know what you would want. I'm going to make you proud, Dad. I'm going to fight so the world can open their eyes and see. I'll carry your name and honor as best as I can, but I will never be you. You were my rock, Dad. Now, I'll try to be." I closed my eyes slowly. A tear fell from my chin to his cold, bruised forehead. I leaned forward and kissed it away. "I'll never forget or stop loving you," I said as I let his hand slip from mine. "Goodbye," I whispered, one last time into his ear.

I stood and turned my back then. I didn't want any other action to mar that memory. I wiped the tears away from my eyes, took a slow breath, and then walked away.

The rest of the week went painfully slow.

The funeral came and I read a bible verse, biting back more

tears through its entirety. My mother and sister bawled and everyone came up, afterward, to console us by offering their kind words.

As we walked away from the church, my brother's fiancée, who had flown in for the funeral, held him. My sister's husband held her. My mother was walked by close friends and family, constantly trying to comfort her as they walked. And for me? I stood alone, staring off into the horizon, alone as always and now more than ever.

There was a gathering at our house, following the end of the funeral, for family and friends. Everyone saw fit to come to me and tell me how much my dad loved me, how proud he was, and how "strong" and "good" I looked. I responded to just a few, keeping my focus on my drinks.

Over the next few days my family left back to head to their respective homes, my brother to Milwaukee, my sister to San Francisco, giving my mother and I the alone time she wanted. My brother had told her that when am immediate family member passes away, armed service members have the option of taking discharge to be with their families and properly grieve, away from the stressful environment that would otherwise be present. My mother begged me to stay. We both needed it, I knew. She was right.

I was faced with a decision now. Stay home, or force myself back to hell in a new platoon, full of strangers and without time to gain control of, or at least, straighten out my emotions. I can say, with certainty, that if everyone knew what Marine Corps boot camp was really like, it would be one-thousand people strong, instead of nearly two-hundred-thousand. After all, why would anyone subject themselves to an experience like that? Pride, maybe? No, the Marine Corps stood for more than pride, I had thought. Worse, why would anyone who knew what I knew, and in my condition, even consider returning to put themselves through it? You would have to be crazy.

And as for my decision? By people who knew me, I had always been called crazy. I held my mother tight, gave her a kiss, and told her I loved her and turned to board my plane back to San Diego, back to a nightmare on Earth, and to leave her behind alone to face everything. I turned to look behind. She was crying hard, face twisted in pain that I had caused. Abandoned by tragedy, and now, abandoned by me.

God, forgive me, because I knew I would never forgive myself.

"There was always talk of espirit de corps, of being gung ho, and that must have been a part of it. Better, tougher training, more marksmanship on the firing range, the instant obedience to orders seared into men in boot camp."
—James Brady, columnist, novelist,
Press Secretary to President Reagan and Marine

CHAPTER TEN

The Return

WHEN HELL TURNS UPSIDE DOWN, AND YOU FIND YOURSELF STUCK IN between Hell and the world you used to know, the hardest part is knowing that life is going on as usual for everyone else on Earth and in Hell.

January 18th, 2002

"You get all your personal issues taken care of?" Kebler had been waiting at the airport when I got off the plane.

I said nothing.

There was no "yes, sir, no, sir, fuck you, sir" that he usually responded with when ignored.

"Everyone's been asking about you every day... We didn't know what to tell them. I didn't think you were gonna come back, but Drill Instructor Staff Sergeant Rand was sure you'd come back."

I said nothing and began to walk to the truck. I stopped, suddenly. Kebler stopped with me and looked, cocking his head to the side in curiosity. "This recruit should have received a very important letter while this recruit was away."

Kebler nodded. "The Senior's been holding on to all your mail and keeping it in his locker while you've been gone. It'll be there."

"Patrick,

Hi, there.

You're already halfway through what must be an incredible experience. Your letters are great and give us some idea of your ordeal. Some are so funny we read them over and over again.

You said a lot of nice things to me your last letter. I'm glad you always understood the choice I had to make and why I chose the path I did, but I regret it all. I wish I could have been there for you every time you needed someone to talk to and I wasn't, but I can tell you this, someday I'll be able to make it up to you by being there for you and your kids. I'll be the best granddad out there.

Well, I'm going to get back to working on the laundry room, I hope you're hanging in there okay. You may be only thinking about the beaches of Florida, but I can only think of seeing you at graduation. I continue to be the proudest father alive.

Love,
Dad."

"Is that it?"

My eyes were wide as I tried to fight a surge of emotions. I had a lump of emotion blocking my throat. I swallowed it down.

"Yes, sir."

We went to the range then, where my platoon was finishing up a week on the field. Czarnecki and Walls saw me along with a few others, who ignored impending punishment, yelled, "Turley!" and ran over to me.

I had written a letter to Derek explaining to him all that had happened, my mess of emotions, and the possibility that I could not continue. I pulled it from my pocket and handed it to Walls. "Make sure Bruckner gets this, will you?"

Walls nodded. "No problem, you okay?"

"I don't know."

Kebler walked back up to me, with Rand closely behind. "We've got to get you back in training now. We don't like doing this, but you missed qualifying on the range. We have to drop you to Alpha company."

"Aye, sir."

Rand walked up to me. "We'll finish this, someday, in the fleet."

I nodded. "I know."

A few hours later, I picked up with my new company. I hadn't seen Derek since he stood across the range yelling, "Recruit Bruckner requests permission to speak to recruit Turley." It would have to wait another couple months.

Kebler drove me up to the Alpha Company barracks and as I reached for the door handle he grabbed my arm and looked at me. I froze.

"Listen, I don't have the words."

What the fuck? "... aye, sir.?"

I opened the door, threw my C-bag over my shoulder, grabbed my alice pack into my arms, and walked up the steps.

"Who the fuck are you?" He was skin and muscle, bald and tall.

"Pick up, recruit, sir!"

"From where?"

"Mike company, sir!"

He furrowed his eyebrows and let his jaw fall a little bit. "How did you get dropped from field week?"

"Emergency leave, sir!"

He asked no more questions.

I spent the next hour unpacking my things. A few of the recruits in my new platoon looked at me, occasionally, with sideways glances. I was a "pick up" recruit. I hadn't bled or sweat with them, yet, and I hadn't been with them from the beginning. They had no desire to talk to me, and I sure as hell did not want to talk to them. I took my shower and got myself ready for hygiene inspection.

"That's Drill Instructor Staff Sergeant Keller." I was sitting down, staring at my boots. "You'll meet Drill Instructor Staff Sergeant Smith, soon. He's a big, black guy, and he's a dick. I'm Walker." He extended his left hand for me to shake. I kept staring at my boots.

"Prepare to mount!" Drill Instructor Staff Sergeant Keller's voice boomed through the squad bay.

Then everyone held their arms in the air and slowly walked to their rack mounting positions. As they walked they yelled, "In the world of many, there are few. These are the ones they call Marines. Warrior by day, predator by night, killer by choice, Marine by God. Platoon one-thousand-thirty-nine, Senior Drill Instructor Staff Sergeant Haney. Discipline through pain!"

"Discipline!" the squad leaders yelled from the corners of the squad bay.

"Through pain!" the rest boomed back.

"Mount!"

"I'm up, he sees me, I'm down!" as they jumped into their racks and lie at the POA.

I was back, back for the hardest part. I realized I would have to manage phase three, and sorting out my own personal issues at the same time. I wasn't sure I could do it, but I knew I would try. The Crucible was waiting for me, and there, and only there, could I earn the pride my father held for me.

It was time to sleep; redoing the beach hump awaited me tomorrow.

It wasn't as bad as the first time. The speed and difficulty were the same, but I was too distracted having conversations with myself in my head. I was going crazy, I was sure, but part of me felt like somehow my father could hear me, so I didn't stop.

It seemed like only a moment had passed when we were done. We dropped our packs and went immediately into our Marine Corps Martial Arts setup.

My partner grabbed a pad and the instructor briefed us to strike the pad as fast and as hard as we could for one minute, until he blew the whistle again.

The starting whistle blew.

I started punching the bag. Scenes started flashing through my mind. *"Relax, Dad. It's not like it's the last time we'll see each other."* *Regret.* I punched harder, my partner was backing up. Pictures of the drill instructors duck taping my hands behind my back and kicking at me flooded my mind next. *Anger.* I punched harder. I was panting when he fell to the ground. "What are you mad at me for? I didn't kill his Dad." *Rage.* I was kicking him on the ground now, fists clenched as tight as they could be, and growling out my mouth.

Someone grabbed me from behind. "Whoa, whoa... who the fuck are you, and what are you doing to my recruit?"

I stood there panting and turned around. A large black man stood before me now. *This must be Smith.* "Pick up, recruit, sir," I said, still trying to catch my breath and my sanity at the same time.

"Ok, 'pick up' recruit," his gold tooth shined in the sunlight when he spoke, "you've got some intensity. Hurt him all you want, just don't injure him."

"Aye, sir."

The day after the terrorist attacks on the towers, Derek and I found ourselves in the Marine Corps recruiting office. The night before, Derek had told me he was going to enlist, and despite my own contemplation, in the moment I just laughed. My fingers twitched like I was still playing with the card in my hand. We would become brothers in yet another way, it seemed.

"Well, well... I remember you. What made you change your mind?" aff Sergeant Smoter asked.

"I have my reasons."

He smiled, stood up and walked over to us. "A lot changed this week. What do you want to know first?"

"Where do we sign?"

The next day was Sunday. Derek and I knew each other very well, so well we knew we could find each other at church. The companies weren't allowed to integrate, but he managed to slide me a letter as I walked past. I nodded to him. It was the best I could do to say, "Be careful, and good luck." He nodded back.

After service, the chaplain called me over to speak with him. "Times must be hard on you, now. But you'll always have strength and be protected if you have faith in God..."

I cut him off, "I no longer believe in God," and walked off.

"Pat,

Well it looks like our plans have changed. About your father, well I think I know you well enough to know that you'll speak about it when you feel like it, and rather than offer a 'Hallmark' statement, I'll just say I'm here to listen and buy the first pitcher when you feel like talking about it. If I was your father, I would be proud of who and what you are.

So we don't get to do the Crucible or say "Oorah' as we step off the parade deck together. They say the greatest test in life is test of time. We sure passed that test, bro. The times, trials, laughs, and everything else have been unique for us.

You are my best friend, Pat, and always will be. Be it five minutes, or five years, I expect our next meeting to be the same. I look up to you like a big brother. Trust, faith and hope are things I afford very few people. You're the only person I can put all of those qualities into, and to be perfectly honest, I thank you

145

for that and condemn you at the same time.

I may have rambled, so be it. It's the truth and I wrote it as it came, but I hope it expresses the resolve that I have. You'll never have to worry about looking to your right and not seeing anyone there.

Your brother,
Derek"

The next day I went back to the range. Early in the morning, Drill Instructor Staff Sergeant Smith took me to the armory for a new rifle, that I would have to set to a new zero. They handed Angel to me. It seemed Rand had given them specific instructions that I receive the same rifle I dropped off exactly two weeks before, and here she was.

Angel.

I wasn't shooting as well as I had, but I was still good. My mind was hazed and every day that I pushed on, I grew more uncertain about what I was doing here. I thought a lot about my mother and what I had done to her. I thought even more about my father. No one else may see it this way, but I had abandoned the both of them in their time of need. Self-forgiveness eluded me. I thought about returning home to try and right, as best I could, what I had wronged. Then I would hate myself for even thinking I could quit. There were people like my father and Derek who believed I could overcome any obstacle and accomplish any feat I attempted. The people who believed in me, after even I had given up. People I would give my life to avoid disappointing and fight with all my will to prove right. I thought I could go no further, but what I thought didn't matter. My new war continued.

Prequalification day came and I shot two-hundred-thirty out of a possible two-hundred-fifty. My new Senior Drill Instructor called for me as we left the range.

"Turley, how'd you shoot today?"

"Two-thirty, sir!"

He nodded. "That's damn good for being home for two weeks. You eat any pizza?"

What's this about? "No, sir!"

"Drink any beer?"

I'm an honest man. "Quite a bit, sir!"

I don't think he was expecting honesty. He looked shocked at first, then smiled and told me to get out of there.

Qualification day came. I could blame it on all the things in my mind. I could blame it on my two week absence. I could blame it on any number of things, but the bottom line is... I choked. I qualified and I only missed Expert by a few points, but in my eyes, I had failed.

"You're not like the other pick-ups." he said.

I was making sure my pack was nice and tight for the eight mile hump that followed the next day. I didn't bother responding, I just kept packing.

"Where you from, Turley?" His name was Zamora, he was double checking his gear for the hump, too.

"All over," I said, jerking down on the straps of my pack.

"I'm from Milwaukee."

I stopped. "Where in Milwaukee?"

"Hartford."

I smiled for the first time since I picked up. "You went to Arrowhead, then. Do you know Becky Crawford?"

He did. As it turns out, my crazy ex had always been crazy.

The eight mile hump had been the easiest one yet. We paced ourselves for the eight miles and moved slowly. I took the time to "talk" to my dad in my head. There were points when the train of recruits had bunched on a hill and we had to run to catch up, but overall it had been a casual stroll.

On the way down one hill, the recruits ahead of me were jumping over something, like there was a large log in our way. When I got closer, I looked down and saw it was a recruit, lying on the ground with a thick mat of blood pouring down his face from under his Kevlar helmet. I just shook my head as I stepped over him.

"Mom,

I just wanted to take a minute and remind you of how much I love you. You mean everything to me, mom. Please never forget that. You'll never know how hard it was for me to leave you, but please understand, I had to do what I felt necessary. Every day and every night I wrestle with my own mind about the situation and what the 'right thing to do' was. I can only hope I made the right decision.

Tell Randy not to worry. I choked on qual day and I too went Sharpshooter. Next week is field week. I won't be able to write for a few days, but I promise I will as soon as possible. Please don't worry about me, mom. I'll always be able to handle myself, but I worry about you. Please do your best to take care of yourself. I'll be home February Twenty-second. You can count on that.

Love,
Patrick"

I had been sleeping like a rock, that night, until a shockwave of pain swept over my right leg. I woke panting and wincing in pain. I tried to move it over and over again... it didn't respond.

No! Not now. Not this close.

"You cannot exaggerate about the Marines. They are convinced to the point of arrogance, that they are the most ferocious fighters on earth—and the amusing thing about it is that they are."
—Father Kevin Keaney
1st Marine Division Chaplain Korean War

Chapter Eleven

Field Week

"Patrick,

I'm sitting here watching the opening ceremony for the Olympics. When it started, so did the tears, once again. It's just amazing to me, what will get me so emotional. Guess it's just another thing dad and I will never get to do together again. I can officially be labeled a basket case, now.

Oh, Patrick, talk to me. It's way too quiet here.

I'm sure you'll do great in the field, and on the Crucible, because you are, after all, our son. I just hope you're busy and don't have too much time to think about dad. All I can think about is February Twenty-second. Take care, honey.

I love you, very, very, very, very much,

Mom"

February 4th, 2002

Something in my leg had gone seriously wrong. Yet, I knew if I went to get checked at medical, my graduation day would not come. MRP, the medical rehabilitation platoon, was a nightmare. You were stuck there until a doctor medically cleared you to be picked up by another platoon until you resumed training. Some stayed months. It was an unacceptable option to me, especially being this close. I started waking up an hour early every morning to stretch and try my best to force my knee to bend. By the time we needed to get going I could barely move... I had a limp, but I could move.

The first day of field week came and went without trouble. We humped out to our camp site, set up our tents, and then humped out to the infiltration course. We covered ourselves in camouflage paint and rushed the course in groups of four, jumping over walls and low crawling through barbwire, guarding the barbwire from your face with your weapon. They had gunfire and explosions going off nearby to simulate a wartime environment. My knee gave me a constant, painful reminder every step, bump and leap I had to take. A painful reminder that showed no sign of lessening.

The night before it had rained, and we had found ourselves low crawling through mud puddles a half-foot deep. When the sun finally rose and dried us up, our cammies were covered in caked on mud clumps that tore at our skin with every movement we made.

With the next day came the gas chamber. The company formed up outside, and one at a time the platoons entered. Each platoon ran out when it was over, choking and coughing, dripping three feet of snot out of their noses, and tears streaming down their faces. There was also the occasional vomiter.

"CS nerve gas—The active ingredient, CS, in one of a group of chemical compounds called lachrymators. These chemicals are tear producing agents, hence the euphemism 'tear gas.' Exposure to them causes severe eye irritation, a profuse flow of tears, skin irritation (especially on moist areas of the body) and irritation of the upper respiratory tract, causing sneezing, coughing and difficulty breathing."

Finally, it was our turn.

I walked in with my gas mask on, eyes shut tight and breathing heavy with nerves. Then the room flooded with CS gas.

Please work, I pleaded to my gas mask.

We had been briefed by the NBC, Nuclear, Biological, and Chemical, specialist of the gas chamber prior to entering. They warned us not to open our eyes, and to try to hold our breath.

"Break the seal!"

We pulled the gas mask away from our faces.

I sat there holding my breath. It was only a few seconds later when I could hear people start to cough and choke. I still held my breath. I opened my eyes to see what was happening, and my eyes began stinging immediately. The room was filled with a pink cloud. The Drill Instructors were walking around with their gas masks on waiting. It was supposed to be one quick minute but it went longer than a minute and I needed air. I tried taking a sharp, quick breath, but as I breathed in my lungs set on fire. After I coughed, I instinctively breathed back in, which set my chest further ablaze.

"Don and clear your gas masks!"

That wasn't so bad.

"Get your gas masks on top of your heads!"

I took a deep breath and slid the face of my gas mask off until it was sitting on top of my head. My chest hadn't had the time it needed to calm down. It was still pounding. It was only a few seconds before I took my next breath of CS gas. I doubled over coughing and gagging on the CS. I could hear a recruit across the chamber screaming as Smith held him against the wall. The recruit was flailing his arms trying to escape and Smith slammed him harder against the wall and "accidentally" knocked his gas mask off the top of his head, sending it falling to the floor.

"Don and clear your gas masks!"

Thank God.

I frantically fumbled to get my gas mask back over my face.

I pushed in on my tab to "clear" the mask and blew out as hard as I could. I could breathe again, but my eyes were still on fire with tears streaming down my face.

"Gas masks out in front!"

We took our gas masks completely off our faces and held them straight out in front of our bodies. My lungs begged for air in between gags. I didn't even bother trying to hold my breath. Even my pores were starting to burn now. I would have to handle it. The recruit Smith held starting going into convulsions.

It's not supposed to be this long.

Senior Drill Instructor Staff Sergeant Haney stepped in the middle of the gas chamber. "Adjust!"

I fought back my choking out of sheer pride. "In the world of many there are few," I began in between coughs. "These are the ones they call Marines. Warrior by day, predator by night, killer by choice, Marine by God. Platoon one-thousand-thirty-nine. Discipline through pain!"

"Discipline!"

"Through pain!"

And it was over.

Later that night, we had our hygiene inspection. We stood online, outside our tents naked, as the January wind whipped through the mountains chilling us to the bone. I was shivering hard.

"Canteens on line, right now!"

Okay, we're going to hydrate and go to bed.

"Canteens over your head, right now!"

Oh, no...

"Dump them on your head, right now!"

The water, like everything around us was nearly frozen. I hadn't thought I could get any colder, until I felt that first trickle of water spill out the canteen and streak down my naked body. I shivered even harder.

At night, we shivered uncontrollably until we began moving. When we stopped our cammies stuck to our skin soaked through with sweat. In the mornings, our cammies came back on, still wet, and we froze until the sun rose. After our cammies dried, the mud would dry and rub our skin raw. The hair rubbed off my thighs and I received a painful red rash in its place.

I felt disgusting. I still had camouflage paint in patches on my face and hands. Every night I found new clumps of mud in the last places of my body I would have ever expected. The only showers we had to look forward to came in the January night out of our nearly frozen canteens, but I only had one day more, and then field week would be over.

We started the next day by humping out to a field and patrolling in fire team formation to a helicopter a few miles away. A fire team formation consists of four people with a good distance between them. We walked slowly and would stop to provide security for each other in areas of visibility.

"I miss you, Dad," I began. I talked to him, or myself, out loud this time until we arrived at the helicopter. I used my sleeve to wipe away the tears still streaming down my face.

That night we humped back down to the rifle range and had our "night fire" exercise.

Moonlight shimmered off the mountains surrounding the range, offsetting the dark tapestry of the sky, and soon, luminous red streaks of light began to sail across the cool night air as we opened fire with our tracer rounds. It was breathtaking.

I served fire watch that night. I spent the two hours shivering and day dreaming about the next day when we could take a regular shower and put on a clean pair of cammies.

"Hey, Harris, get dressed, you've got to be on in fifteen minutes."

"Okay," he called back.

I was exhausted. Sleep didn't come often in boot camp, and it came even less for me with the nightmares that now haunted me. I dreamed of being there when he died, and he would look up at me say, "Patrick, help..." and I couldn't do anything. The "good" dreams were the worst. I dreamed of being older with kids and a beautiful wife, and my father was there... he was there playing with my children. Those were the hardest dreams. Those were the dreams of what should have been but would now never have the chance of becoming reality.

It had been fifteen minutes.

"Harris, get up!" I was angry now.

"Leave me, alone. I'm sleeping!"

I tore the flap of the tent open and dragged his sleeping bag out into the center of our "tent-city", as he scrambled to climb out.

"What's wrong with you, man?"

I cocked back, and punched him in the face. He spun to the side and caught himself with one arm, cupping the other to his mouth while it spilled a thin line of blood.

"You're late," I told him, nostrils flaring.

He nodded, still holding his mouth, and I went to sleep.

"I, Patrick Turley, do solemnly swear that I will support and defend the Constitution of the United States against all enemies, foreign and domestic; that I will bear true faith and allegiance to the same; and that I will obey the orders of the President of the United States and the orders of the officers appointed over me, according to regulations and the Uniform Code of Military Justice. So help me God."

With one raised right hand, and a simple paragraph, we sealed our fates.

The hardest part of enlisting had been telling my parents. I had to drink before hand to relieve some of my nerves. I knew the hopes they had for me and my future, and that they didn't involve a low paying and dangerous line of work. When I told them I had enlisted, they begged me to tell them I had joined the Airforce or the Navy. When I told them I had chosen the Marines, the phone went silent aside from my mother's sobs. When my brother, a former Marine, found out, he just laughed and replied with, "You'll see" when I asked what he was laughing about.

Derek and I had already begun to make our preparations. Sending our belongings to our parents and taking written and physical tests. Unsure of how long we would be gone, we tried tying up loose ends by saying goodbye to the people we cared about.

Derek glanced over at me as he drove, his expression thoughtful. "It'll make you feel better if you see her before we go."

"Just keep driving."

My father was in town on business. We spent our last day having dinner with him... he was so proud.

"Relax, dad, it's not like it's the last time we'll see each other."

As soon as we stepped foot back into our squad bay, Smith grabbed me and pulled me to the quarterdeck. "I got you now, Turley."

"Aye, sir!"

"Push-ups!"

"Push-ups, aye, sir!"

"Puuuuuush-up!"

"Marine Corps!"

"Exercise!"

"One, two, three, one, sir! One, two, three, two, sir..."

"Why is Harris' face all fucked up?"

I stopped and jumped up, popping immediately to the POA. "This recruit punched him, sir!" I dropped back down. "One, two, three, three, sir!" I yelled as I continued pushing.

"Get up."

I popped back to the POA before him.

155

"You think you're a bad ass?"

"No, sir!"

"One-thousand-thirty-nine is a tight, good platoon. A platoon is a team. All you've done is beat up some recruits." He paused, thinking to himself. "Do you want to be a squad leader?"

"No, sir!"

His mouth tightened with displeasure. "Mountain climbers!"

"Mountain climbers, aye, sir!"

It was almost over now. The pain, the struggle, the testing, all over. Only one obstacle remained before we made our trip back south to the recruit depot to prepare for graduation. The Crucible.

"Mom,

Sorry I haven't been able to write for the past few days because I was in the field. Believe me, you have been on my mind. Tonight I leave for the Crucible. I'm not sure of what to expect, but I'm nervous. Something happened to my knee last week and it barely works right now... I don't even want to know what kind of shape it is going to be in when I get done with the Crucible, but as long as I get to see you on February Twenty-second, I can take the pain.

I really wanted to get a letter from you today to help motivate me while I'm gone for the couple days, but they didn't have any mail for us. I hope you're doing okay, Mom. If not try doing what I do and focus on my graduation. Then I'll be there, and at least for a little while, things will be as 'alright' as they can be.

Thinking of you always. Wish me luck.

Love,
Patrick"

"The Marines I have seen around the world have the cleanest bodies, the filthiest minds, the highest morale, and the lowest morals of any group of animals I have ever seen. Thank God for the United States Marine Corps!"
—Eleanor Roosevelt, First Lady of the United States

CHAPTER TWELVE

The Crucible

February 14ᵗʰ, 2002

I'VE HEARD A LOT OF PEOPLE GIVE A LOT OF VARYING OPINIONS ABOUT the Crucible, but the facts remain. Two hours of sleep a night, and two and a half meals for two and a half days of heavy activity. You humped nearly fifty-miles, only stopping to do activities that drained you further still. By the end of the Crucible approximately a quarter of all recruits are broken.

The Marine Corps officially describes the Crucible as "The Recruits' Final Test: For 54 straight hours, recruits' endurance, teamwork and skills will be pushed to the limit. Through perseverance and courage, they will finish as platoons and earn the title Marine. During The Crucible, recruits face obstacles that must be negotiated as a team, day and nighttime marches, night infiltration movement, combat resupply and casualty evacuation scenarios, combat field firing as a team, minimal food and sleep, simulating combat, leadership tests, and core values training."

We started out hard. I had been selected to be in my Senior Drill Instructors squad. A month ago, I had wanted to and volunteered to go with Rand's squad. But circumstances had changed drastically for me.

We humped out to a site, broke into pairs, and then each of us carried his partner on his shoulder for a mile, swapped positions and headed back. My knee was on fire.

We found ourselves at three red circles next.

Pugel sticks.

I suited up and the fight started. After a couple neutral hits, I managed to bump my opponent back and followed by delivering a "killing blow". Then I ran to the next circle. Pugel sticks is draining. You have an adrenaline rush for a few seconds and then it gets replaced by tired, burning muscles. The second match took longer. We spent a minute knocking into each other with the middle of our sticks until I finally twisted the tip of my "bayonet" into the side of his helmet. I panted as I stepped into the next circle. I lifted my head just in time to see my opponent charging toward me and thrusting the tip of his stick in my helmet. I fell back several feet, the pugel stick dropping from my hands, and landing with a thud.

I lost?

The exercises went on, and in the afternoon we arrived at yet another site called "Mackie's passage", in reference to Civil War Medal of Honor recipient Corporal John Mackie. It was a tire suspended in mid-air by two ropes, painted red on everything except the hole in its center. The red meant death. Death meant dragging Fred, a one-hundred-fifty pound dummy, for a mile.

"Your squad is aboard a sinking ship. The only way out is through this porthole," Senior Drill Instructor Staff Sergeant Haney said, gesturing towards the suspended tire. "Turley, take charge!"

" Aye, sir!"

"Alright, listen up, this is how we're going to do it..." I designated two people to lift Walker first and feed him through the hole in the tire to safety on the other side. Now, Walker could help other recruits when they came halfway through, and so we fed

159

our squad through the hole until Zamora and I were the only ones left on our side.

"Go," he told me. "I see you limping... I'll drag Fred."

I wanted to, but I shook my head. It may have only been an exercise, but it was symbolic and it was my job to make sure everyone got to safety. If anyone fell, it had to be me.

"There's no way to get through that, don't be stupid."

"I got it," I assured him. Zamora then put his hands forward as I picked him up and carefully placed his feet through the tire. Walker grabbed his feet at the other end and steadily pulled him through.

"Thirty-seconds!" Haney yelled.

My mind was racing... *how can I do this?*

"Twenty-seconds!"

"Hurry up, Turley!" they yelled to me.

I took a few steps back and did a handstand and slowly dropped my feet halfway into the tire. Walker grabbed my legs.

"Not yet!" I yelled, holding my position. "On three... one, two, three!"

On three, I pushed off the ground with my arms, and my stomach lit on fire as I used its strength to keep myself parallel to the ground while Walker pulled me through by my legs.

We did it.

After that, my squad had decided that Walker, Zamora and I would be the focal points for the rest of our activities. Even though I was only five-foot-eleven inches, and currently one-hundred-seventy pounds, I was strong, mentally even more than physically. The squad chose me to be one of the "big" recruits the smaller ones climbed on to accomplish the missions. I ate little, trying to ration myself for the next day, and as the day wore on, I grew incredibly tired.

Finally, the sun set. It was time to wait for our night activity...the ammo re-supply hump. It was only a little over three miles, but we had to carry eighty pound ammo cans in pairs along with our gear we already had on. The metal handles on the ammo cans would dig deep into our hands as we moved out, shoulders straining to carry the weight. Even though we paused to swap sides, both of my hands started to bleed, and rotating sides became irrelevant.

Day one had gone well. We had both worked and persevered as a team, and were all on a natural high knowing everything would soon be over and we would be going home. Day one ended for two brief hours and day two of the Crucible began.

I had taken a bottle of one-hundred-and-twenty acetaminophen pain killers from home, and had it stashed in my LBV, load bearing vest, pocket since field week. With the searing pain in my leg, I was already down to forty pills. My knee was getting harder and harder to move. My back had stiffened from shouldering the weight of recruit after recruit. My legs burned from chafing. My entire body ached. I was starving and tired.

MRE's, meal ready to eat, are disgusting, but on the Crucible they're a delicacy. We woke up that morning and moved out immediately. By late morning, we finally stopped and dropped our packs for our next event. I found a rat that had been decomposing for at least a week next to the plates we staged our packs on. I started to drool.

"Don't even think about it, Turley," Haney warned.

We were at another infiltration course. This time they designated a few of our smaller recruits to be casualties and become limp so the rest of us could drag them through. Barbwire slapped me in the face as I dragged Harris by the back of his LBV. There was no love lost between us, so not only did he go completely limp, he also fought back as subtly as he could. I wrestled him up to his feet, hoisted him up on the wall and then pushed him off to land four feet down on the other side. He became much easier to handle after that.

When we finished the course, we dropped our LBV's and transfered into MCMAP, the Marine Corps Martial Arts Program. I was paired with Tanner, a big kid from Michigan and our first squad leader. I had to lay down as he straddled me and shoved the pad into my face attempting to smother me as I fought back with elbow strikes. I kept him at bay with my elbows until it was time to switch. I held the pad and when the whistle blew, frustration got the best of me and I shoved it into his face and began to slam his head into the ground as he fought back with his forearms in vain. and then we moved out, again.

Day two our morale dropped. We forgot about how close we were to finishing and were overcome by exhaustion and hunger. Saying "we fell apart" would be an understatement. By late afternoon we were performing an event where we had to carry ammo cans across an imaginary lake over cables. I suggested we carried them in teams of two, and treated it like the "slide for life", but each recruit would keep a hand on the ammo can as they shuffled across.

"That's the stupidest fucking idea I've ever heard." His name was McGregor, our third squad leader, the one Smith wanted me to replace.

We didn't have the time for this, and more importantly, by this time, we didn't have the patience. Our tempers were firing on all cylinders at this point. The exhaustion, the hunger, and the cumulative frustration of several months of Hell was coming to a head here.

"McGregor, ever since we started this shit you haven't lifted a finger to help, so stay out of it!" I snarled. My own open emotional wounds didn't help my presence of mind.

"You know who you're talking to, recruit?" he yelled back, getting in my face.

"You might be a squad leader, but you're not shit here. So back up, boy." I pushed him.

162

He pushed back. "Or what? I'm not Harris, you can't just..."

I grabbed him by his LBV and threw him to the side. He fell and skidded back. Walker grabbed me as I stepped forward. "Let it go," he told me.

I breathed and nodded, recomposing myself as quickly as possible. "Alright, let's do it."

Haney just watched.

The weaver. It was an obstacle from the Confidence Course that they had brought to the Crucible. The weaver from the Confidence Course was only about eight feet tall. This one was at least fifteen. It was a pyramid of logs spaced evenly with a few feet separating each one. You had to go over one log, and under the next. If that wasn't hard enough, in addition to the size increase, we now had to carry ammo cans with us.

I found myself, yet again, at the heart of another obstacle.

It was when I had made it nearly to the top and about to begin my descent when Zamora went to hand me an ammo can across the log. I reached for it, and suddenly my body grew heavy. I pulled my hand back instinctively and stared back at him like he had somehow done something to me. My lungs pounded harder and harder every second and I could feel my blood burn through my veins.

And then everything went black.

I could feel my abdomen convulsing violently as I threw up into the toilet. Derek was behind me, laughing at me as he relaxed, watching "Band of Brothers" on HBO.

It was the night before we left town for boot camp. After having dinner with my father, we had gotten a ride down to the Milwaukee MEPS, "Military Entrance Processing Station," where they had given us a room at the Best Western across the street.

It wasn't nerves that had me vomiting in the toilet, it was the bottle of vinegar that I had been forcing myself to drink all night.

We had been told one of the first things we would be required to do upon arriving at boot camp would be to take a drug test. Stupid party. It had been nearly two months since that party, and I wasn't even sure if drinking vinegar to flush your system really worked or was an urban legend, but after all this hassle, I wasn't taking any chances. I wiped my mouth off with a wad of toilet paper, glared at the one liter bottle of vinegar, sighed to myself as I picked it up and raised it to my lips, and finished the rest.

Derek laughed harder as I leaned back into the toilet.

I wouldn't be sleeping that night.

Derek's family had met us at the Milwaukee airport the following day to say goodbye before we boarded our flight to Chicago, preceding the subsequent connecting flight to San Diego. The day before, my father had asked to come, but I had told him not to. I didn't like goodbyes. And I didn't view our departure with any significance.

Of course back then I hadn't realized it would've been one last opportunity to see him again. An opportunity, in hindsight, that I'd give anything for.

When I came to, I was laying on my back alongside an ammo can while everyone was standing around me, I had passed out, knocked the ammo can down as I fell from the weaver and landed on top of it, ribs first.

Thank God I was wearing that flak jacket.

"You alright, Turley?" Haney asked, hovering above me on one knee.

I nodded my head as Zamora helped me up. My ribs were aching and my neck was sore from the fall, but it could have been a lot worse.

I continued devouring pills as we humped further and further, but it wasn't working anymore. The day was too long. We were meeting the rest of the squads for our night activity brief and we were early.

164

Haney took us on a run to kill time. I tried as hard as I could to keep up for the first lap, but I fell to the back of our squad.

"Some of you want to move slow, huh? Move out!"

No... no...

I fell out for the first time, limping as fast as I could behind the platoon. As they went for a third lap, my face squinted in pain as I hobbled harder and harder to try to catch up.

I fell out?

The night activity went smoothly. We did the infiltration course, again, only it was dark this time. None of us were really paying attention to the course. Between the cold, and our heavy eyelids we couldn't think about much, and the thoughts we did have were dominated by one thing... the Reaper.

We would sleep for another two hours, and when we woke, we would face our last and greatest challenge... the Grim Reaper.

Fire watch always gave us a one-hour warning to morning. I knew how taxing the Reaper would be, so before I slept, I made the decision to wake up an hour early, stretch my knee out, properly pack up my gear, eat the last meal I had saved, and wait for hell. The warning never came...

One moment I was asleep, and the next our tent had been torn away from above us and Smith stood there screaming. Our Drill Instructors had told our fire watch that we would have an extra two hours of sleep to prepare for the Reaper so they could catch us all by surprise for our final push. I had, luckily, slept in full uniform. I struggled to scramble to my feet, falling twice, to pack my gear. I was one of the first to finish, and I ran with my pack to our formation, trying to tear open my chicken-with-salsa meal as I ran. The bag opened and the chicken breast fell to the dirt. I stopped to turn as Keller stomped on it.

"Go," he said to me.

Starving, exhausted, and injured, I obeyed.

My feet were covered in blisters. As we started to move out, and begin our final hump, I could feel them pop and begin to soak my socks in puss. Between my feet, the new ache in my ribs, and the ever-present lancing pain firing through my knee, I reached into my LBV and pulled my bottle of painkillers free. I had nearly thirty left, but within ten minutes the bottle was empty.

We were winding through the mountains for at least an hour now, and slowly my pain was winding down and shifting into delirium. It had been about three miles when we came back to our campsite. A lot of us buckled under pure frustration. Cries of frustration flew everywhere, and some burst into tears.

There I was, worn to the point of unconsciousness, when my chest started to shake. My jaw fell, slightly, and the corners of my mouth turned into a smile as my chest shook. *I'm laughing?* I couldn't do anything else. Maybe it was the pills. Then again, maybe I could appreciate the hilarity of twisting our emotions well past their breaking point.

"Let's go!" they yelled.

We pushed forward.

Occasionally, I was aware of the pain searing through my feet and my leg, but none of it seemed real. I felt like I was merely a spectator, watching everyone else go through hell. As time wore on, recruits were falling out and dropping like flies. I would grab their rifles as they dropped behind to help them out. I had collected three, and my own, by the time we stopped at the top of the mountain.

We were formed up again, surrounded on our sides by steep cliffs and nearly in the clouds. To our front were crudely built shacks and houses to simulate urban warfare that I would later come to know as "combat towns".

Is it over?

I paused, waiting for myself to answer. I knew I had taken a few too many pills. Maybe even a lot too many.

This is it. That was the Reaper. It's over now.

I sighed in delirious satisfaction.

166

"Step it out!"

It wasn't over. It had been right in front of me. To my left, rather. A massive mountain on top of a mountain and one of the steep cliffs that I couldn't imagine could be part of the hump. But it was. *This* was the Reaper. As we took our first steps onto the Reaper, all sense of formation died. It was so steep you could stick your hand out in front of you and touch the ground. My chest was heaving, and I had become extremely light headed. Thankfully, for the most part, the pills were working.

"Amazing Grace..."

The singing was coming from next to me. I turned my head to find the source, and Hernandez looked back at me. He had been one of the few people from my new platoon that I had liked. I nodded.

"How sweet the sound," I joined, as we struggled to climb further, side by side.

"That saved a wretch like me."

I grunted, struggling to make my knee bend to the terrain's demands.

"I once was lost..."

Hernandez's foot slipped and I reached out to grab a hold of the frame of his alice pack until he steadied his footing.

"But now am found... was blind but now I see."

We struggled forward together and after convincing myself I was not, in fact, about to die nearly ten times, we reached the summit. We didn't speak a word to each other... we couldn't. It was so beautiful. We had climbed so high, you could look to either side and see clouds of mist shrouding the rolling landscape we had just conquered.

Conquered... We had *conquered* it all. Everything that been thrown at me, I had accepted, defeated, and here I stood, at the top of my new world. The National Anthem started to play, and it all seemed worth it.

"*Mom,*

It's over. I can hardly believe it but it's over. February Twenty-second I'll get to see you. February Twenty-second I'll get to hold you. It's all over mom. Don't write any more letters... they won't get to me in time. I'm coming home, mom. I'm coming home.

Love,
Patrick"

"Hell, these are Marines. Men like them held Guadalcanal and took Iwo Jima. Bagdad ain't shit."
—Marine Major General John F. Kelly

CHAPTER THIRTEEN

Loose Ends

February 16th, 2002

THE "WARRIOR'S BREAKFAST," THE PRIZE AT THE END OF THE CRUCIBLE is a celebration of cheap steak, cheese eggs and whatever other breakfast foods available, it is a mildly upgraded "continental breakfast." To each of us, it was delicious. With each fork-full, I tried to stuff more and more food into my mouth until I gagged.

The pain-killer "delirium" I had been experiencing was fading. The pain that had faded into submission grew back stronger than ever, but it was over. The Crucible was over.

It was a journey that triggered every possible emotion. Fear, pain, anxiety, frustration and hatred to elation, fellowship, pride and victory; I had felt it all. The mounting anxiety I had held for so long towards that event... it was now gone. It was an experience that I will never forget.

As I walked out to join the platoon in formation my stomach lurched. I leaned over and threw up on the ground. I wiped my mouth with a sleeve and moved on.

"Hey Pat,

Hopefully, you'll get this before you graduate, but we haven't gotten mail in a while, so who knows. I hope you're hanging in there with Alpha Company, this will be over for you soon. I tell ya man, I miss ya. Sundays aren't the same and I really don't talk to anyone anymore. It really sucks not being able to see you react to Rand . . . he never quits.

A week or two ago, Bequet was on fire watch, he saw that all your things had been cleared, so he actually tried to take some initiative. Just as Rand is 'tucking' us in, Bequet goes over to your rack and starts tearing it down like he's gonna fold it. I break from the POA, down the Drill Instructor Highway and as I'm about to lay that fat fuck out, Rand gets a hold of him, gets him against the windows for a moment or two and says 'Don't you ever touch his fucking linen again, you fat piece of shit. You'll never be good enough to even touch his rack.' So I guess you were right . . . maybe he did like you.

Well bro, take care like I know you will. My thoughts are with you and your family.

Your brother,
Derek"

"You think it's over, huh?" Smith yelled across the squad bay. "You think you've done the Crucible, so you deserve to be Marines? Fuck it. I'll bet you already think you are Marines. You're wrong. Footlockers on line, right now!"

The games continued, but I didn't care. I couldn't care. It was almost over and I was going home.

"What's the matter with you, Turley?" Smith asked, cutting off my path. "Are you sick or something?"

My tray had a single slice of bread on it. I was pale. Ever since the Crucible, I had thrown up nearly everything I had eaten.

The pills had done something to my stomach.

"Yes, sir."

"You need to eat. Go get some food."

"Aye, sir."

I grabbed a scoop of chili macaroni from the recruits working the line and sat down.

"Here," I told Zamora, while I slowly chewed on my bread. "Eat this."

"Are you okay?" he asked, quickly scooping the chili mac onto his plate while Smith was distracted.

"I'm fine."

As soon as I walked outside, I doubled over and vomited chunks of half digested bread and stomach bile dotted with spots of blood.

Today was our PRAC test and I could barely stand.

"Turley.." It was Smith.

I forced myself to the POA. "Yes, sir!" I managed to respond.

He looked me up and down and stood there, slightly bobbing his head forward and back as he thought. "Tomorrow you go to Medical. I've seen you limping. Check on that shit, too."

"Aye, sir!"

"But, that's tomorrow and today is today. When I see a chit saying you're sick, that's one thing. Until then, you're feeling fine. Now get your ass in formation and quit marching like you just got fucked in the ass and making look like shit, or I'll break that fucking leg off myself."

"Aye, sir!"

I almost fell as I turned to run to my platoon, but I didn't. We took our multiple-choice written test first. It was one hundred questions on everything from heat stroke to the war in Korea, significant events in Marine Corps history, and appropriate first-aid reactions. Things that had been drilled into our heads from arrival and that we should have a firm grasp of at this point and. I missed one. Then we broke into our practical application.

I could still disassemble and reassemble the M16A2 service rifle faster than most, no matter how dizzy I was.

"LMGAS. Lightweight, magazine-fed, gas operated, air-cooled, shoulder fired weapon, sir!"

"What's this?" one of my examiners asked, holding a picture of a chevron with three stripes up, crossed rifles in the middle, and two rockers down.

"Gunnery Sergeant, sir!" This was too easy. I'd lived the life for the past three-and-a-half months, and prided myself on how far I'd come. We all did.

"What's a Master Sergeant?"

"Master Sergeant, E-eight, three stripes up, crossed rifles in the middle, three rockers down, sir!"

"Good to go, recruit."

And on it went. I had been anxious about performing a hasty "fireman's carry" due to my weakened condition, but with some minor struggling, I made do. PRAC was over now, and soon the rest would disappear with it.

"Oh, you're a cute one, aren't you? Take your glasses off for a second, would you?"

"Aye, ma'am," I responded.

She smiled back. "My name's Christine, not 'ma'am'. What's your name?"

"Recr..."

"No. What's your name?"

"Patrick..." It felt like I was greeting an old friend as I breathed out my own name. It had been so long since I had been treated nicely, I didn't know what to do. I wonder if all the Navy was as nice as Christine. And if so, how?

"Alright, so what's wrong with your knee, Patrick?"

"Everything."

I spent most of the day sleeping while they ran test after test on my knee. Finally, Christine sat me down with a concerned look on her face.

"Patrick, you have ligaments that are ripping as your kneecap is pulling away from the bone, if you want to get better, you're going to need surgery. I'm going to give you bed rest for tomorrow, and Wednesday we'll take you to the Hospital and see how many months we need to hold you here."

I nodded and left, limping back to my squad bay.

"What'd the doctor say, Turley?" Smith asked.

My bed rest chit was crumpled up in my pocket. "This recruit is fine, sir!"

Smith nodded.

Smith held me back from final drill and the final PFT as he watched me grow sicker.

I want to participate. I have a lot to offer the platoon towards winning the events, at least I had *something* left to offer, right?

"'No,sir'? You're lucky I don't have your ass for that. You're hurt, no sense making it any worse."

A few weeks ago, being hurt wouldn't have mattered. Now, with our character and strength proven, and the end in sight, they had lightened up, if only a little. Maybe he even liked me, I thought. A little bit, maybe? No, that wasn't it.

I performed inspection arms flawlessly and returned to the POA as the Master Sergeant inspected me grabbed my rifle. My bearing and body locked and my eyes burned a hole into his forehead.

It was the Battalion Commander's inspection and our last chance to fail in becoming a Marine. We were dressed to kill in our Alphas. The only thing missing, our Eagle, Globe and Anchor, the symbol of the Marine Corps, would come in just a few short days. Senior Drill Instructor Staff Sergeant Haney had warned us about this Master Sergeant. Despite this inspection being more of a formality than a chance of failure, he was vicious.

He took my weapon, shifting it around slowly for better sunlight, meticulously inspecting every detail. "Weapon's bone dry. No dirt, no carbon." He looked at me evenly. "Good to go, recruit. Outstanding work on your weapon." Of course I took good care of Angel. He stepped forward closer to hand me my weapon. My hands shot out and gripped it tightly. I fired my right hand to the muzzle so I could assume a proper "order arms" and continue the inspection. My inspector was shorter than me and standing too close. When my right hand shot up to the muzzle of Angel, it sent his campaign cover flying two ranks away.

Haney's eyes went wide.

The Master Sergeant stood there, slowly seething underneath his stoic bearing, waiting for me to flinch, or my eyes to widen, as I maintained my bearing and proceeded to bring myself to the order arms. After a deep breath, he calmly walked over, picked up his campaign cover, and resumed his position in front of me. He took one more deep breath before exploding into me.

"Do you not like me, recruit?! I don't like you! I hate recruits! I used to be a Drill Instructor, you know that?! I'll kill you, boy!" He paused and stared at me while I calmly stood, stone. "Why'd you knock my cover off?"

I had been mulling my response to this inevitable question over in my mind since I had committed the action and continued to do so during his tirade. I took a deep breath and replied, "This recruit refuses to compromise the rifle manual of the United States Marine Corps to accommodate the height of this recruit's inspector, sir!"

Two months ago, I would have been trembling with fear and uncertainty. Now, I stood before him with confidence and discipline, prepared and eagerly awaiting his next move.

"Are you aware of the acronym JJDIDTIEBUCKLE, recruit?"

"Yes, sir!"

"What does it mean?"

The question he had asked the others recruits hadn't been

nearly as difficult. Still, it was something every Marine *should* know, and in a few more days I *would* be a Marine.

I took another deep breath. "Judgment, justice, dependability, initiative, decisiveness, tact, integrity, endurance, bearing, unselfishness, courage, knowledge, loyalty, and enthusiasm, sir!"

"What is BAMCIS, recruit?"

And another deep breath. "BAMCIS, the six troop leading steps, sir! Begin the planning, arrange for reconnaissance, make the reconnaissance, complete the plan, issue orders, and supervise, sir!"

He nodded. "I hate to admit this to you, recruit, but you're pretty good to go. I look forward to you serving my Corps," he said before walking off.

I'm really good, I thought to myself, barely managing to keep my smug self-satisfaction internal. I stood there, at the parade rest, beaming. I viewed these inspections as an opportunity for me to exhibit my superiority and today, yet again, I had done just that.

The Battalion Commander, Lieutenant Colonel Chase himself, was making rounds in our platoon now, escorted by Senior Drill Instructor Staff Sergeant Haney and stopping at every third recruit. As luck would have it, I fell in his path.

Inspection arms, I commanded myself and then performed without any discrepancy.

Lieutenant Colonel Chase took it from me, and after a clumsy feigned inspection of my weapon, handed it back to me. He looked at me and smiled. Smiles were not something shared by his enlisted predecessors, but regardless, this man had earned a level of respect I doubted I could ever match.

"Good morning, recruit."

"Good morning, sir!" I boomed back at him.

"Do you know who I am, recruit?"

"Yes, sir!"

"Who am I?"

"First Battalion Commander Lieutenant Colonel Chase, sir!"

"Good," he said back, nodding. "What do you feel was the hardest part of recruit training, recruit?"

I'd listened before while he heard a myriad of responses. From the Crucible, the Reaper, the gas chamber, being IT'ed, to even Swim Week, he'd heard it all… but he hadn't heard from me yet.

"The hardest part of boot camp for this recruit was this recruit's father's death, sir!"

His eyes went wide and "Jesus" softly escaped his lips, before he quickly recomposed himself. "Did you get to go home, recruit?"

"Yes, sir! This recruit was previously with Mike Company and returned with Alpha Company after the funeral, sir!"

"Have you been seeing your Senior Drill Instructor and meeting with the Chaplain to talk?"

Had I pressed it, I have no doubts that the opportunity would have been afforded to me, but I could neither imagine talking to my Senior Drill Instructor about my feelings, or even requesting time to see the Chaplain as we battled through our third phase. I answered with, "This recruit has had no need for special attention, sir!"

"Is your family coming to graduation?"

"Yes, sir!" My mother and sister, at least.

He nodded again. "They have a lot to be proud of in you. Welcome to the Corps, Turley."

"Aye, sir! Good morning, sir!"

"Good morning," he said back as he walked off to continue his portion of the inspection. As Haney passed, he leaned in close and whispered, "I thought you were going to shit your pants when you knocked the Master Sergeants cover off."

For just a moment, a slight smirk crept across my face.

"Remember this?" Haney asked, pointing down towards the rows of yellow footprints on the ground before us. "You ran off the bus, with a bunch of Drill Instructors yelling for you to do things you didn't even understand yet."

Remember?

Derek and I had landed in San Diego late in the evening on November Fourteenth. We had to check in at the airport USO and everything was arranged from there. I was nervous. These were our last few minutes of freedom, or free will for that matter, for another three months.

"Have some coffee, bro," Derek said, handing me a cup. "I have a feeling we're going to need it."

I nodded and took a slow sip. I hadn't slept more than a few hours the night before and we were both too anxious to sleep on our flights. We didn't hold high hopes for any sleep that night either.

"You ready?" I asked, my eyebrows perked.

"Doubt it," he said back smiling. "You?"

I shrugged. "Probably not."

We weren't. Not even close.

Can you be ready for something like this?

There were dozens of us gathered at the USO, and we all piled onto a bus a half an hour later. The drive had been short... too short. Before we knew it, the bus doors opened, and the world went silent. My eyes widened and my pulse quickened as the slow, determined footsteps brought the campaign cover clad Drill Instructor closer and closer into view.

"My name is Drill Instructor Staff Sergeant Jones. Welcome to thirteen weeks of hell." He paused, taking in a deep breath. "Now, *get off my frickin' bus!*" he yelled, exploding at us.

I jerked myself up and made a sprint for the door, as we all pushed and fought through each other for the very first time.

There were other Drill Instructors waiting outside around a set of yellow footprints. I stood on a pair of footprints as the others fell in around me, oblivious of where Derek might be.

"Stand at the friggin' POA!" one of them barked at me, with a sharp finger pointed into my face.

What the fuck is a POA?

And so it began. We were immediately stripped of our clothes and belongings and had our head shaved.

My three-and-a-half months had just begun.

"You've come a long ways from the boys you arrived as, and you have a lot to live up to. Tomorrow you walk onto the parade deck one last time as recruits and walk off Marines. Don't disappoint us."

We had yearned for and awaited these weapons so badly when we had arrived. Now, nearing our completion, we yearned for our release from them. For me, it was yet another bittersweet moment in a several month long chain of them. On one hand, I was losing a large burden. On the other, I had to "say goodbye" to Angel for the very first time.

"There goes a pain in my ass," Zamora said after handing his weapon off to the armorer.

"Well? Give it up, recruit!"

I had been standing there, in a daze with my thoughts. I nodded and let go of Angel.

Goodbye, Angel. I'll miss you. I wasn't sure if I was talking to the weapon, or finally seeking closure with the woman.

"Some people spend an entire lifetime wondering if they made
a difference in the world. But, the Marines don't
have that problem."
—Ronald Reagan, President of the United States

CHAPTER FOURTEEN

Graduation

February 21st, 2002

IT WAS A DAY I HAD LOOKED FORWARD TO EVEN BEYOND GRADUATION. The night before I had barely been able to sleep, despite my exhaustion, due to the excitement my mind held towards the day I had now awoken to. The anticipation welled stronger inside me every passing moment as I came closer to seeing my mother again.

It would start with a four mile "Moto Run", or motivational run. My knee was hurt, and I knew running would aggravate my injury, yet I knew my mother would be there, watching for me. With all the pain I had endured to arrive to this day, going through a little more for pride in my mother's eyes, would be no problem.

Keller stood there smiling as we changed into our PT clothes. "Now remember," he began, "No matter how cool you, your family, your girlfriend, or whoever thinks you are for going through Marine Corps boot camp, you're still about to look like a fag in those shorts."

It was the first time we all laughed together.

The company formed up in a line and before us stood our families. I could hear my mother yelling, "Patrick!"

"Stop smiling, Turley," Senior Drill Instructor Staff Sergeant Haney whispered out of the corner of his mouth.

It almost made me want to broaden my smile or even laugh, but not yet.

The Seniors called out, "Adjust!" one at a time to their respective platoons. Finally, Haney called upon us.

"In the world of many, there are few. These are the ones they call Marines. Warrior by day, predator by night, killer by choice, Marine by God. Platoon one-thousand-thirty-nine, Senior Drill Instructor Staff Sergeant Haney. Discipline through pain!"

"Discipline!"

"Through pain!"

"Riiii-ght *face*!"

Our heels slammed together with authority.

"Forward, march!"

Initial drill, final drill, they couldn't have held a candle to how we performed now. The excitement, the anticipation, the pride, it all resonated inside us and we felt, at last, truly accomplished.

"Double time, march!"

And off we ran.

The run had been slower than our others, thank God. Even so, my knee strained with every step, but I reveled in pride as we ran to motivating cadences for the first time.

"Hey Army, where are you going? Get in your tanks and follow me. We are Marine Corps, can't you see? Hey Navy, where are you going? Get in your ships and follow me. We are Marine Corps, can't you see? Hey Air Force, where are you going? Get in your jets and follow me. We are Marine Corps, can't you see?"

My knee had held up great until we stopped. When we halted and I slammed my heels together, my knee erupted in pain. I ground my teeth as I stood at parade rest, my mother and sister watching me from somewhere in the assembled crowd of prideful families and friends. It hurt badly, and we turned to run back to the squad bay, I kept up in the formation limping along as fast as I could.

Once back at the "house" I showered and threw on my Charlies as fast as I could.

"What's the rush, Turley? Last day, savor it," Zamora said with a smile.

"We're late for the ball, Cinderella," I said back, pulling my zipper up.

After all, we had a ceremony to participate in. We were about to receive our Eagle, Globe and Anchors. We were about to become Marines.

After the band finished playing, we marched straight in to the parade deck and turned to face the bleachers. My mother and sister were in those bleachers. I had decided to wear my glasses for the ceremony. I knew how awkward I looked with them on, Derek had given me constant reminders at every opportunity, but more than anything else, I wanted to be able to see my mother. The anticipation we all held toward this very moment had me, and everyone else, nearly giddy. Yet it was an exhibition of what we had undergone, how much we had grown, and what we had become, so we held our bearing and stood sharper than ever before. We settled in and snapped to the parade rest.

Our First Battalion Commanding Officer, Lieutenant Colonel Chase, took the microphone. "I'd like to start by saying 'good morning' to the family and friends of the selfless men standing before you today. The sacrifices they have made to protect our great nation have not been small. Over the past three months, these men have undergone the most physically and mentally taxing trial the United States, or as I believe, the world today has to offer. Through that training they've evolved with a lasting bond, skills, and the knowledge that will help them overcome the challenges of our great nation, and in doing so, they have become warriors; warriors of the mind, body and soul. Now please excuse me as I turn to address the men of Alpha Company. Alpha Company, in just a few moments your Drill Instructors will present you with the coveted Eagle, Globe and Anchor. At that time, you will become a United States Marine. Drill Instructors... take over."

"Parade... *rest!*" Haney called.

I'm not sure what song the band was playing right then, but it was beautiful. Everything about the moment was beautiful. One rank at a time, the Drill Instructors moved down the squads. After just a few minutes, Kebler stood before me.

I popped to the POA and he simply smiled as he placed a small, black Eagle, Globe and Anchor into my palm. I took my cover off and began to unscrew and insert my new symbol of pride into it. A swirl of emotions ran through my body. I took my time, savoring the moment I had worked toward for so long and so hard.

"Throughout their stay here at Marine Corps Recruit Depot San Diego, they have been referred to as 'recruit' and only 'recruit', but never 'Marine'. I'd like to be the first." He turned to face us. "Good morning, Marines."

We snapped to the POA. "Good morning, sir! Oorah!" The bleachers shook and then erupted with cheers as we popped back to the parade rest.

Our Battalion Commanding Officer continued, "Over the course of their enlistment, they will find themselves in many unique and challenging situations, but the skills and discipline they have learned, and will retain, will carry them through even the most challenging obstacles that life has to offer. Without any further rambling, to the loved ones gathered in attendance today, I present to you your United States Marines! Drill Instructors, take over and carry out the plan of the day."

It's coming. I can't believe it's finally here.

The bleachers were erupting in cheers as one by one the platoons of Alpha Company were finally dismissed. And finally it happened.

Haney wheeled an "about face". "Platoon, atten-*hut*! Platoon one-thousand-thirty-nine... *dismissed!*"

We all took one step back in well practiced harmony.

"Aye, sir!" I screamed, not even bothering to halt the smile forming across my lips.

In perfect unison we performed our about face. "Oorah!" we yelled, and for the day, that was the end of it.

Our families burst out of the bleachers to see us and my heart raced as I searched through the throng of my new brothers and their families for my own.

"Patrick... Patrick!"

I jerked my head to the left. It started off distant but quickly grew stronger. And there she was. The nerves, the anticipation, it all heightened my senses and I felt free. There were so many things I wanted to say to her as she walked towards me, her face red and convulsing as tears began to streak down her pretty face. So many things I had to say, but I found myself unable to speak what I wanted to as I grabbed her in my arms. I could only whisper, "I'm sorry." She didn't hear me. I'm not certain I even managed to say it out loud. It didn't matter. All the work I had done, all the effort I had put forth, all the pain I had endured was for this moment alone. Nothing else mattered. It was only seconds, but while I held my mother nothing else in the world even existed.

She took a step back and looked at me, wiping the tears from her eyes. I took off my glasses and smiled. She squeezed my hand and forced a smile back.

"How does it feel, Patrick?" my sister asked.

How does what feel? I had been very proud during the ceremony, bursting with emotion, but the actuality of the event hadn't even dawned on me. *I'm a United States Marine now.*

"I don't know... it hasn't really hit me yet!"

I put my glasses back on. My sister laughed hard and even

my mother chuckled a little. I smiled sarcastically and nodded.

"I know, I know. Let's get something to eat. We've got *all* day."

There was a buffet at a restaurant on base by the waterfront. My Drill Instructors were there, so after warning my mother not to speak with them at all costs, I hid as best I could to actually enjoy my meal. I was careful to use silverware properly. I was careful to maintain correct posture. I was careful about everything.

Curiosity naturally overcame my mother and while I went back to the buffet for fifths, she made her way over to my Drill Instructors. She had told them she had been worried about me after my father's death, only to be reassured that they were surprised I returned and that I had been very strong.

Drill Instructors spend so much time as an antagonist of your life that it's hard to realize the underlying role they are actually performing. They had a job to do. They had to break us down to rebuild us in order to make us unbreakable and to serve our country with pride. They had to make men capable of performing tasks that couldn't be charged to anyone else. And they performed their jobs diligently with extreme prejudice.

My mother, sister and I spent the day shopping at the base exchange. Anything that bore the word "Marines" or "USMC" did not escape my mother's clutches. Today I wasn't sweating or bleeding. I relaxed, as best I could, and ate. I ate burgers, French fries, pizza, ice cream and anything else I could get my hands on.

The day went by fast and I said my goodnights to my mother and sister and headed back to the squad bay. It was shortly after we had all returned when Haney called us to the quarterdeck.

"This journey started three months ago, and in just three short months your world changed forever. When you go home, you're going to notice things are different, but the only thing that changed is you. Your friend pumping gas, living in his mom's basement won't seem so cool anymore. *We* are here for a greater purpose. The Marines protect the world, which is why we've been so hard on you. The brass will never understand why we do what we do. They don't like it. It can save your lives, and more importantly, the lives of others."

He was right.

He slowly looked us all over. "We've taken on a lot of new faces. Turley, you had a lot to prove coming back, but you did, and you're all one-thousand-thirty-nine."

I nodded when he addressed me. I had a lot to prove, but one-thousand-thirty-nine? To me, one-thousand-thirty-nine had felt like a means to an end. In many ways it was all the same, and I had made friends and accomplished my goal at their side, but deep down I still felt attached to three-thousand-thirty-nine.

"You've all done good, and you're now Marines." He paused, his face tightening. "I'm proud; keep it that way."

"Aye, sir!" a roar rose from the squad bay with the exception of one, "Oorah!"

Haney froze. "What the fuck, Walker? You're still in my house. Start pushing!"

Some things will never change.

We hit the Chow Hall first thing in the morning on Graduation day with our newly ironed on Eagle, Globe and Anchors worn proudly on our cammies. Instead of the usual, "eggs, recruit" and "aye, recruit" banter, we heard, "aye, sir."

For the first time, there was no rush.

"Momma, momma can't you see, what the Corps has done to me. Put me in a barber's chair. Snip, snip, I had no hair."

We were walking to stage our gear by the parade deck so we could make a hasty exit after graduation. Drill Instructor Staff Sergeant Smith led us out one final time. This time he led us not with "ATT" but with proud cadence.

"I used to wear my old blue jeans, now I'm wearing cammie greens."

185

It was a special memory to me.

"I used to drive a Cadillac, now I'm humping with my pack."

To me, it signified the death of the pain, and the birth of the brotherhood.

A faint whistling of the Marine Corps Hymn started to fill the base theatre.

"From the halls of Montezuma, to the shores of Tripoli. We will fight our country's battles on the air, on land and sea. First to fight for right and freedom and to keep our honor clean. We are proud to claim the title of United States Marine." The voice came from before us now. It was a large black man, grinning while he sung. "Our flag's unfurled to every breeze, from dawn to setting sun. We have fought in every climb and place that we could take a gun. In the snow of far off northern lands, and in sunny tropic scenes, you will find us always on the job, the United States Marines." He waved us in and slowly we all began singing along. "Here's health to you and to our Corps, which we are proud to serve. In many a strife we've fought for life, and never lost our nerve. If the Army and the Navy ever look on Heaven's scenes, they will find the streets are guarded by United States Marines."

I smiled, filled with pride.

"Good morning, Marines."

"Good morning, sir!"

He shook his head. "No, no, Devil Dogs. 'Good morning, Gunny'."

"Good morning, Gunny!" we yelled back through broadened smiles.

"We all know that song, right?"

"Yes, Gunny!"

"Let it be a source of pride, and a guideline for you. It means everything and you've made it. You've done it all and don't let anyone cheapen the experience of what you have accomplished in these months. You're going to get out to the fleet, meet soldiers and sailors. They'll think they're your peers. Wrong. We have no peers. 'If the Army and the Navy ever look on Heaven's scenes, they'll find the streets are guarded'... by who?"

"The United States Marines!" we finished.

"By *us*. So if they attempt to trip you up, just start whistling and walk away." He turned around and casually started whistling the Hymn again. "If the Army and the Navy..."

The theatre shook with applause as he walked off the stage.

We were standing in formation when Zamora, next to me, kneeled down to vomit.

"Oh man, not now... It's graduation. Get up, Zamora."

Haney ran back and pulled Zamora from the formation.

"Forward... *march!*"

And so it began. We marched out and stopped all the way across the parade deck. The color guard came out, presenting the Marine Corps and United States' flags, and then the band. I was concentrating on the future already. In another hour or so, I'd be on the road home. *Just a little while longer.*

Lieutenant Colonel Chase stepped onto the parade deck. "You're now a part of the world's most respected fighting force, and America's nine-one-one force. When you look at the Eagle, Globe and Anchor, remember your core values of honor, courage and commitment, and think of those that came before you and carry on that tradition of pride and excellence. On behalf of the base commander, Drill Instructors, and other personnel on the recruit depot, congratulations and we look forward to serving with you in the future. Good luck, God bless you, and *Semper Fidelis.*"

This was all bittersweet to me. I had struggled for so long, and come so far, but the man who I really wanted to be here, who I really wanted to witness this, was not. Nor would he ever know. Never again could I give him a reason to feel pride. Never again would I be able to justify to him his belief in me. Maybe somehow and some way he watching and was proud. I didn't quite know what to feel.

"Riiiight, *face!*"

"Forward, *march!*"

We wrapped around the parade deck as the announcer welcomed high ranking military and government visitors and spectators. As we came in front of the bleachers with our gathered families and friends, Haney called, "Eyes right!"

We snapped our heads forty-five degrees to the right, still marching forward. The bleachers cheered. We finally halted in front of the bleachers and the honor-men, or guides, were called out and retired the guidons with the drill instructors. The guides fell back in to their respective platoons and the Senior Drill Instructors were given the command to dismiss us once and for all.

"Platoon one-thousand-thirty-nine, *dismiss!*"

"Aye, sir! Oorah!"

I held my mother again after the ceremony had ended and took one last look at the small part of Southern California that had caused me so much pain and yet left me with so much pride. I didn't cry as I looked over the Drill Instructors and new Marines that had played such an instrumental role in my life. Tears were not for them. Tears were for my father and my father alone.

"Do you want to say goodbye to anyone?"

I shook my head. "I'll see them soon... Let's just go, mom. Let's go."

My fight, my struggle, my war, had been for my father and nothing else. I had won in his name. I stood tall... hoping some where, somehow, he was there, smiling down on me and proud to call me his son.

I smiled. This adventure was over, but the game of life that been paused for three and a half months was about to resume, and I knew I could play again.

Epilogue

WHAT MAKES A "MAN"? A SIMPLE WORD ON THE SURFACE, YET WITH so many underlying allusions beneath. An image of strength, responsibility and perseverance shrouding the personal pain, fear and weakness that lies within us all. In right and wrong, being biased by culture, environment and perception, there are rarely any definitive answers. The mirror tells no lies. What others see is usually quite different than the story your own face can tell you as you gaze into your reflection.

The world, a myriad of limitless possibilities, keeps turning, and with it, so do our lives. Our lives, a string of experiences, undergo waves of "ups" and "downs" as we swim through an ocean of unanswered questions. The "ups" may make our lives worthwhile, but it is the "downs" that define them.

Sometimes, it feels like the only things that are truly certain are pain and death, and the only things left to turn to are hope and faith; hope in the future and faith in, if nothing else, yourself. Who are we?

Who am I? In the mirror I see it all: regret, pain, weakness, hope, faith, and strength. It all breathes inside me, inside us all. Who am I? A man proud of my decisions, proud that I stood up for what I believe. I am proud that I persevered through harsh circumstances and trials, of the Marine Corps for its history and for doing what is necessary to make rough men willing to protect the American way of life at *any* cost whether it bends, or sometimes even breaks, the rules set in place by frailer men who could never understand.

The experience is one I value more than any other that I've had in this life. Though I served with honor, there are countless braver, *better* men than I that made sacrifices for us for which we can only dream. I feel privileged to have been able to serve at their side, and uphold the standards and traditions to the best of my ability.

The few. The proud. The Marines.

Those Who Did it

The Bright Side:

I WENT TO BOOT CAMP IN SAN DIEGO, CA. YEP, I'M A "HOLLYWOOD" Marine, too. A quick over-view of the surroundings is in order here for those who have not attended MCRD, San Diego. On the backside of our Barracks there was a "Practice Grinder" (parade deck) where we conducted close order drill every day. On the other side of that Grinder, was a row of WWII era Quonset Huts used for Recruit Training (hereafter referred to as "ovens," because by noon, that is what they were) running out like fingers from the practice deck. On the other end of the ovens was a road that we used to run on for PT that ran all the way down the row of ovens, and on the other side of the road ran a five-foot-deep ditch with a twelve foot high fence on the other side topped by concertina wire. Most important to the story though, is the runway for San Diego International Airport on the other side of said fence. All day, every five to ten minutes of every day, Freedom Birds leaving SDIA

The Platoon was at the end of our final week of the "First Phase" of training, about week five. We would be departing for Camp Pendleton for our two weeks of rifle range training and then two weeks of field training in a couple of days. Life were beginning to settle into a rhythm. One of the patterns that emerged was the regular assignment of me and my fellow squad leader; recruit Hemler, to rifle guard duty during classroom time. These classes were held in the "Ovens." Leave it to the Corps to try and hold classes right next to a runway! There wasn't enough room in the "Ovens" for all of the recruits to take their M-16A2s in with them, so platoons would "stack arms" outside in a column. Rifle guards were then posted at each end of the column, facing each other, and were supposed to guard the weapons with their faces stuck in their Marine Corps Knowledge (the recruit Bible of all things Marine Corps). Hemler and I each had a couple of years of college and were among the older members of our platoon, so I guess they figured we could read and catch up. As luck would have it, I had my back to the runway that afternoon.

Hemler wasn't so lucky. About fifteen minutes into a one hour class, I glanced up to see Hemler watching airplanes taxi and take off and over his shoulder, just coming into view at full quickstep. A Hat. "Hats" are what Drill Instructors are called by the Marines of MCRD that are not DIs. The Hat refers to the distinctive "Smokey the Bear" campaign covers worn by DIs and shooting coaches in the Corps. This was no coach, and he was sporting Gunnery Sergeant chevrons as well.

Not good.

Have you ever tried to yell with nothing but your eyes? I did. I tried. Not a chance in hell that Hemler would have heard me over the 747 he was fondly watching take off. Not a chance in hell I was going down with him either. The last thing I saw was Hemler, eyes right, watching that big old bird banking left with a pair of elbows sticking out from right behind him as the Hat had assumed the classic hands on hips, chin out, light up recruit stance. Recruit Hemler stood 6'7" and skinny as a bean pole. Our series Chief Drill Instructor, Gunnery Sgt Garcia, 5'6" and built like a member of the Mexican Mafia had a voice that sounded exactly like Cheech Marin.

"Soooooooooooo, you like those there Freedom Birds, do you Recruit?" bellowed Gunny.

I swear I saw Hemler's feet jump a full foot in the air. "Sir, No Sir!" yelped Hemler.

"Oh, so now I am a liar...eh, Recruit?" Hemler was a dead man.and he knew it too. Gunny was smiling.

"Sir, no, sir!" Hemler yelled out over another jet taking off.

"I tell you what I'm going to do for you, Recruit. I like you," (bad, bad, bad sign) "in fact I like you so much, I'm going to help you out," smiled Gunny. "I'm going to let you chase those Freedom Birds, and if you can catch one, I'll let you leave and I won't tell no-one!" Gunny roared above another jet preparing to take off.

"Sir?" a puzzled Hemler replied.

"GO! RUN! GO! GO!" Gunny ordered (grinning from ear to ear the whole time).

Off Hemler flew across the parade deck, past the Ovens, and down the road. The plane roared down the runway and was airborne.

"Too slow, too slow, get back, get back, get back!" Gunny called to Hemler.

So back to us Hemler ran.

"Oh, look. Here comes another one!" laughed Gunny, and off Hemler went again… and again… and again. After all was said and done, recruit Hemler chased five jumbo jets that afternoon, and didn't manage to catch a single one. After returning from the fifth one, Gunny looked up at Hemler who is standing at attention, soaked in sweat, and trying not gasp for air and says "Damned recruit, I thought you had it in you to catch you a Freedom Bird. Too bad, but hey, I got an idea. We're headed up to Camp Pendleton next week. I'll come and find you and we'll see how you do with Helicopters! They aren't as fast as them damned Freedom Birds, but they are sneaky bastards. They'll jump right straight up in the air on you! But I like you Recruit, and I think you just might have it in you to catch one of them! Now get your face in your Knowledge where it belongs!"

"Sir, yes, sir!" barked out Hemler and Gunny Garcia left us trying not to laugh out loud.

Later that night as we were getting ready for lights out, Hemler was laughing so hard he had tears coming out of his eyes, "Two months ago I was a Junior with a 3.5 GPA in Electrical Engineering at Purdue, today I am a Marine recruit chasing airplanes!" We cracked up about it for the next couple of weeks and forgot all about it.

Gunny did not.

On the morning we were to Hump a 20 mile forced march to Mount Motherfucker, later called the Reaper, we were gearing up to get online, and a voice suddenly loomed: "Where is my Motherfucking Freedom Bird Recruit?!"

Hemler's face went white, then he stood up, grabbed his gear, asked me to keep an eye on his squad while he was "playing games with Gunny," grinned and called out, "Sir, here Sir!" and he was gone.

We could hear Gunny laughing and talking to everyone about how they were going to hunt Helicopters. About three quarters of the way to *Mount MoFo*, at our bivouac area for chow and training we heard the unmistakable sound of a UH1 Huey helicopter coming in. It landed in a field a quarter of a mile from us and who gets out of it? None other than recruit Hemler, grinning ear to ear. Hemler would later tell us that Gunny drove him quite a ways in a HMMV explaining to him how you catch a Helicopter the whole time. As they rounded a corner, there they sat, a whole row of them and one of them was starting up! Hemler looked at Gunny, who grinned back, told him "Be careful, remember they are sneaky Bastards!" and sent him off to catch the one spinning up the rotors. When he got there, the crew strapped him in and took off!

As Hemler made his way from the LZ to our Platoon, Gunny Garcia joined us from out of nowhere. "Goddamn Recruit! You got no luck whatsoever!" Gunny roared, "I get you on a perfectly good helicopter, I don't tell no one you are gone, and the goddamned thing brings you right back to your fuckin' platoon!" He turned to the rest of us. "Ain't that about the worst luck you ever heard of, platoon?"

"Sir, yes, sir" we all barked, trying not to laugh.

"I think God is trying to tell you something, recruit. I think God wants you right here with your Brothers, so they can take care of your sorry ass...because your Karma stinks, Recruit!" He laughed.

"Sir, yes, sir," croaked Hemler with a grin.

And with that, Gunny was gone

—Dave Smoot

Boot Camp was honestly three of the funniest months of my life. The creativity the DI's showed in messing with people was hilarious, as long as you weren't the target of that creativity.

The end of the first week with our permanent Drill Instructor Team, on our first Friday night, fire-watch for 0400 was assigned to two little guys from Portland, OR. I can't remember their names as the DI's just called them "Frick and Frack." They looked like they were twelve. These two had signed up on the "Buddy Program" and both needed height wavers to get in. Five foot even, the both of them. The 0400 watch had the dubious responsibility of waking the DI on duty at 0430 so he in turn can have the platoon up at 0500.

It didn't happen.

"Frick" went to the Duty Hut hatch and barely knocked on the wall and squeaked, "The time on deck is 0430, sir."

He did it again at 0445… and again 0500.

At 0510 the Duty Hut door exploded open, and Sgt Miller (our DI… in PT shorts) proceeded to explode himself as he informed us, in no uncertain terms that it was time to "GET THE FUCK UP!!!!!" then vanishes into the Duty Hut and re-appears in about 5 min fully dressed and looking like he'd just been standing inspection (how DID they do that?). He calls for the offending Frick (who is by now shaking like a leaf and looking even younger than a twelve year old). Sgt Miller snatches the fire-watch's cheap Timex from Frick and barks, "Can you not fucking tell time?"

"Sir, yes, sir!" came the reply.

"Well not loudly enough! Get in that shit-can! NOW!"

Well, Frick wasted no time hopping into the trashcan. Sgt Miller gives him the upside down lid and proclaimed that he is now a "Shit-bird Coo Coo Clock."

He bellowed "Recruit, I want you down in that can with that lid over you like you got a spring hooked to your ass... NOW!"

BANG! Down goes Frick. Then Miller booms, "Anytime I hit this can, you will explode up and they better hear the time on deck at the main gate! You will then get your bird ass back down in that can like you still have that fucking spring on your ass!" He then hauls off and kicks the shit out of the can. Frick explodes into view and informs the world that it is now 0535 at a much more enthused volume and, WHAM, he's back in the can. Sgt Miller kicks the shit-bird Coo Coo clock at least 4 times in the next 5 min, chuckling to himself every time he does so. At 0550 Sgt Miller bellows, "Get on the road for chow" and whoosh, out the hatch we fly and form up in platoon formation for head count. The end result? One missing and you guessed it... Frick.

Just as Miller is sending Frack to "collect the Coo Coo of our shit-bird clock" there comes a sound from the squad bay. Clang! "SIR THE TIME ON DECK IS 0600, SIR!" It turns out that the Series Chief DI was wandering through to start inspecting the squad bays and bumped the can. Time froze for a heartbeat. Frick then comes flying out and gets online red faced as a beet. Miller didn't hesitate, gave us a right face, and we stepped off for the Chow Hall and never looked back to see Gunny come out of the squad bay white as a ghost! We all heard Miller telling the story to the rest of the DI team that night in the Duty Hut and they were laughing their asses off!

—**Sgt. Jeff Moore**

There are so many boot camp memories it's difficult to concentrate on just a few. I spent my time at MCRD San Diego during the summer of 2002, which was right around the time Austin Powers was at its peak. We had a big guy in my platoon, probably 6'3" 260 lbs. He wasn't fat though, just a home grown farm kid. In another platoon in my company there was a guy who was maybe 5' tall with boots on and 110 pounds soaking wet. The drill instructors made the big recruit chase the smaller recruit around just like Fat Bastard was trying to eat Mini Me in the movie yelling, "Get in my Belly" and Mini Me squealing "eee, eee." The entire platoon got a kick out of it, but the DI's always get the last laugh.

Our first week up north at Camp Pendleton where our DI's would say, "You're mine up north bitches," one recruits parents thought it would be a wonderful idea to send the platoon seventy-seven candy bars in the mail. The Senior DI passed out the candy bars while we were all on line. They gave us fifteen seconds to get as much of the candy bar in our mouths as fast as we could. What he didn't say was that after the fifteen seconds we had to spit every drop of that candy bar out. I doubt a handful of recruits even got to swallow anything at all.

Desperate times call for desperate measures right? Well what do you do when you're at boot-camp, bored with no alcohol? You get drunk off of Listerine, duh. That's what four recruits in my platoon did. Yes, they were rolled back the following day (Author note: Guess we lucked out)

Who puts their wallet in their pants pocket during final drill, seriously? The few personal belongings you keep stay in your footlocker pretty much 24/7, for my platoon anyway. So for 11-12 weeks of boot camp nobody had wallets on them, and what day does some douche bag decide to put his wallet in his blouse pocket where it's easiest to see? Final drill. We are standing in formation, stiff as boards, waiting to be inspected. The DI walks up to this guy and immediately see's his wallet. The DI is completely flabbergasted that this recruit has his wallet in his pocket during final drill. The entire platoon knew we were royally fucked as far as winning final drill, which was the ONLY competition we even had a mild shot at winning.. The look on our bulldogs face when the inspector found it was priceless.

The last week of boot-camp the entire company went to a San Diego Padres game. Each recruit was able to take out $40 to use at the concession stands. This was no accident. For two plus hours every recruit in the company ate everything they could. Krispy Kreme's, pizza, hot dogs, nachos... etc. Before we even left the stadium, guys were throwing up from gorging themselves. Once we returned back to base where do you think the first place the DI's took us?

The Chow Hall.

Every recruit got a plate, and of course it had to be full. Nobody got up until their plate was empty. I can't remember anyone not throwing up.

—Sgt. Jeff Moore

"Left, right, left, right, left. Platoon… Halt!"

"Step freeze!" we answered back in unison.

Marine Corp boot camp is a series of drill, class, drill, more drill, PT, drill, drill again, cleaning your rifle, chow, drill, drill and finally, drill.

At this particular moment my platoon was on the Parade Deck at Parris Island, S.C., executing Platoon Drill movements. On the Island female recruits often train away from their male counterparts except when drilling. This morning such a female platoon was marching across our front.

At this point, I had been on the island for 3 weeks and was starting to forget what a women looked like. One of these recruits despite her nasty cammies and butch hair cut looked damn good and caught my eye. I followed her as her platoon marched past mine. I stared too long.

THUMP! Came the sound of one of my drill instructors open hand driving into my chest.

"Recruit fucking Larkin what the fuck are you looking at?! Eyes front you fucking idiot!" my drill instructor yelled, spit flying haphazardly from his mouth.

With lips quivering, not because I was scared, which quite honestly would be bullshit because I was terrified , but because I didn't see him coming and was caught off guard. "Ye... Ye... Yes, sir!"

My Drill Instructor leaned forward so the brim of his campaign cover is touching my forehead, his eyes piercing into my very soul. I mean into my fucking soul. Those eyes were terrifying. "What the fuck were you looking at!?" he screamed. Then, in a low terrifying voice so only I could hear, "Were you starring at one of those nasty fucking cunts over there? Were you looking at one of your female fucking recruits? Did you forget to fucking jack off last night, recruit?"

Reflexively, I yelled back, "No, sir!"

His eyes widened. "Oh, so your whacking it after lights out, are you? Did I fucking tell you, you could fucking play with your shit?" he asks like he actually wants an answer.

"No... Yes..."" I paused in frustration, losing my bearing. "Fuck," I breathed.

I was fucked then and I knew it. I was in a catch twenty-two and I fucking knew it. The best play here was to shut up and hope the Drill Instructor gets bored of you, like a cat will eventually tire of a ball of yarn, and walks away, or better yet one of your fellow recruits laugh. After all, if it's not you it's pretty funny and the Drill Instructor that hears that bearing dissolve away in laughter will proceed to destroy that fellow recruit.

Unfortunately, this time there came no laughter... and he didn't get bored.

"Well which one the fuck is it recruit?" he asked, his veins beginning to pop out of his forearms.

"Yes, sir?" I said. But saying anything in boot camp is another no. You scream everything if you want to stay safe.

"Oh, so you disobeyed a direct fucking order then didn't you? Good," he says as if he was the devil himself.

He calls out to the Senior Drill Instructor, "Senior Drill Instructor, recruit Larkin wishes to engage in individualized instruction in the pit."

"He does, does he? Well oblige him," my Senior barks from his place along-side the platoon.

My drill instructor begins to smile as he looks at me. "You heard the Senior. Thank him for granting your request and run your ass to my pit."

I'm fucked. I take off running and scream while I do, "Thank you Senior Drill Instructor, sir!"

It was only a few minutes that I found myself in the pit, basically a gigantic sand box, and already at the brink of exhaustion. I had performed countless diver bombers, diamond pushups, Marine Corps pushups, leg lifts, jumping jacks, mountain climbers, I hate mountain climbers, and then I had my arms fully extended rifle in hand.

"Fifth general order," my Drill Instructor barks.

"Sir, this recruits fifth general order is to never leave my post unless properly relieved, sir!" I barely manage to yell through heavy pants.

"Position of attention, move," he barks.

I snap to attention, breathing heavy from my nose, a mixture of sweat sand running down my face.

"I'm watching you recruit Larkin. Now get back in formation with the platoon and you better fucking run."

"Yes, sir!" I scream before sprinting back to the parade deck for a few more fantastic hours of drill.

200

As I am running it dawns on me I have ten more weeks of this bullshit. It was then that I asked the question that every Marine Corps recruit has asked themselves since its birth: What the fuck was I thinking?

To all my fellow brothers in arms, and especially to my fellow *MARINES, OORAH AND SEMPER FIDELIS*

—Sgt Liam Larkin

One funny thing my head drill instructor used to do is make where we were from into some homosexual reference. For example, when asked where I was from I replied, "This recruit is from Buffalo, Sir." He replied with some comment like, "Oh, you mean you're from Butt-Fuck O'lo." Then there was the guy from Okla-homo...

—Sgt Michael Brady

Now that I think of it, I remember when i got my rifle for the first time but I had to take a piss. The drill instructors wouldn't let me or my friend go because we kept messing up the proper way to ask to make a head-call. So without controlling myself, I pissed in my pants while I was getting issued my rifle. It was embarrassing, but everyone understood my pain.

—Sgt "Steve-O"

I always wondered what they added in the chow to make all of us not think of masturbating. I swear I didn't whack off until we got back from Camp Pendleton about 2.5 months later.

—Sgt Christian E

I grew up like any typical American. I used two hands to eat. I quickly learned this is a big no-no in Marine Corps boot camp. You get to use one utensil, one hand, no eye contact or talking to anyone, and about 3-5 minutes to eat. Time and again there were punishments for those who couldn't handle the one hand rule, often times it was "GET OUT!" Because this rule was strictly enforced I was transformed into a speed eater. I can now kill just about any meal in about 5 minutes.

During the Crucible, the 3 day culmination of boot camp, there are many exercises that flex your brain as much as your muscles. For some, the muscles are stronger than the brain. I had the opportunity to see what happens when logic is abandoned and it's a battle of strengths.

One of the exercises that we had to over come, was designed with 3 planks, a sand pit with wooden post, and about 30 feet to traverse to get to the other side of the pit. The planks were different sizes which force the recruits to work together to get from one side to the other. Luckily in my group, we had a "He-man" that was able, or thought he was able, to muscle over the thickest and heaviest plank. In an instant He-man found out that he had made a grave mistake. As his muscles gave out, the plank quickly fell. The next thing I saw was, at that time, the most graphic thing I'd seen. He-man had caught his finger between his plank and another. His finger was peeled like a banana. The tip of his finger was intact, but from the knuckle up, was stripped of flesh as it dangled like a popped balloon. So much for common sense.

Growing up playing sports, I was used to having to hustle and sometimes wait in line to use the bathroom before the game. In boot camp, the only difference was that you had someone in a campaign cover yelling in your face to "HURRY UP!" The other big difference was that if you had to take a shit, there was no door on the stall and you had a line of devil pups staring at you as you try and pinch one off.

For most of us, this was a new experience and some weren't sure how to handle it. Some held their shit all day and snuck off to the head in the darkness of the night, others dropped it in a

202

porta-shitter if possible; but for most, you had to sit on the throne with an audience. This was probably the most uncomfortable things I had to deal with in boot camp and the first time I blatantly had a dude meat gaze as I drop a steamer. With his eyes fixed on my junk, I looked straight at him and said "DUDE! WHAT THE FUCK!" And like a guy being caught staring at a woman's tits, he went deer in headlights and looked everywhere but at me.

—Sgt Eric Crook

That guy tried to fight SSgt Barkley during rifle maintenance

I remember it happening, but didn't see it. We had the first floor squad bay behind the Parade Deck stands. We were outside doing Rifle Maintenance when I heard some feet shuffling and a "plop." I looked up and saw this skinny black recruit being held back by 3 other recruits, SSgt. Barkley's Smokey is on the ground. SSgt. Barkley and SSgt. Diaz are in the kids face. Senior Drill Instructor SSgt Scott comes out of the Squad bay, breaks it up and takes the skinny black kid off. By the time we came back from chow later that afternoon, the kids rack was bare and the footlocker was empty. We never saw him again

Stupid ass Nelson used the Drill Instructors washer and drier in the middle of the night. I remember waking up in the middle of the night to a Drill Instructor yelling "WHY ARE YOUR CAMMIES IN MY WASHER!" I remember saying, ah crap, tomorrow is going to suck, then going back to sleep.

The next day, we hit EVERY pit in front of the Chow Hall, had chow, then hit the pits behind the Chow Hall until at least 3 people threw up.

This happened at the WW2 History class (this was in 1997, so pre 9/11 era).

The instructor comes into the class and announces that this morning a dirty bomb had been set off during the morning rush hour in New York. A 3 square mile area of New York was inhabitable, and the number of dead and wounded is not known. Saddam Husain has already taken credit for the attack.

He went on to say that a number of our Drill instructors have already been recalled to the fleet so they can be deployed. As a result, we would only have 2 DI's for what remained of our training.

He then added that the next morning we would be moving up to Edson Range to qualify with the rifle and complete a 2 week Infantry course. After completing that, we were going to be deployed to Iraq to kick Saddam's ass. No graduation, no Boot Leave. If we survived the war, when we returned, we would be sent to the appropriate MOS school.

He then stated that before all this can happen, they need to know who the Conscientious Objectors were. Therefore, if you had a moral or religious objection to killing someone, you needed to stand up and move to the wall.

With tears streaming down his face, our platoon GUIDE is one of the FIRST Recruits to stand up and move to the side.

Our Senior DI, SSgt. Scott, marched down the aisle, ripped the arm band off him, snatched the broken-down gideon off the desk, marched to the back of the class where he threw the gideon against the wall, snapping the spear.

SSgt Diaz running around the platoon with his NCO sword yelling "Let me stab one, Senior. Just let me stab one…"

Ssgt. Diaz was our "Junior" DI, and we were his last Platoon before he recycled back to the fleet. He was a 5'4" ball of muscle. He was from Guam and had a thick accent, so it was sometimes hard to understand him.

The first time I remember him doing this was when we were practicing Colum left and rights. He was at the Pivot Point raising his sword when we were to pivot, and dropping it behind us. Well, we kept screwing it up, so he would run into the platoon and let tear into whoever screwed up.

Well, after screwing up 5 or 6 times, he started to tell us that he was going to stab the next one to screw up. At this point, we were only 2 to 3 weeks into our cycle, so we honestly thought that if Senior said it was OK, he would stab us! We also did not know that a NCO sword was so dull it could not slice warm butter. Inevitably, we screwed up and he ran into the platoon and smacked the recruit that screwed up with the broad side of the sword. As this went on, he would also smack the recruits around the "screw up" for letting him screw it up!

I remember him doing that again, before Final Drill. We kept dragging our feet on "Change Step" so he threatened to stab us again. But this time we knew better and were not buying it. At some point he ripped the cover off of some recruit's head and stabbed it. I remember him holding up his sword with the cover sliding down the blade yelling, "NEXT TIME IT WILL BE YOUR FACE MAGGOT!

—**Rick Valdes**

The Darker Side:

I was in Platoon 1073 in Delta Co. 1st RTBN and we were at the rifle range. It was the Friday before Columbus Day and it was our Qualification day. It must have been after lunch when we got to the 500 yard line. I was sitting on the ammo crate that we used for seats while keeping score for the recruit that was on the firing line. From my left I heard a recruit ask the other on the line "Is your weapon on safe?" The recruit on the line casually looked back while still in the prone position and was like "Yeah" and then started to look down range again.

Just then the recruit hopped off of the ammo crate and ran down and got in front of the firing line. He put his mouth on the other guy's rifle and reached down with his hand and switched it off safe. At first I thought he was like blowing air into his rifle before I realized what was going on.

One round went through his head and I saw the "Pink Mist."

205

I stood up and yelled "Cease Fire." When I got to the line the guy's head was at the bottom of the little berm at the 500 and his feet were at the top. His feet were shaking really bad and I looked at his head and blood was pouring out of his ears like a broken sprinkler. I was going to give him CPR but when I went down I saw some thick purple shit leaking out of the back top of his head where the hole was. I knew that he was dead. By this time the range coaches and DIs were yelling for everyone to get down and put their faces in the dirt. It felt like I was down there for hours. My senior Drill Instructor came over to me and told me to get up. I was still in shock and he gave me a hug and I started crying. It sounds kind of weird but I cried for about 30 seconds and then CID came and took me to their office with about four other guys. They offered us Cokes and stuff but I declined. They asked us what we saw and stuff. After the chaplain came in and talked to us for a bit.

It turned out that the guy that killed himself was the Platoon Guide for the Platoon downstairs from us. He had done well at everything so far at boot camp. He unq'ed (unqualified) that day, and I guess the pressure from his DIs, as well as the Range Coaches got to him and he couldn't take it.

— **Jeramy**

I had pneumonia for the last 5 weeks of boot camp. My senior drill instructor Nick named me "Cancer" on the Crucible because I looked near death the entire time, and forced me to go into medical when it was over. Since I was so sick of being in that place, I figured I would rather risk death by pneumonia to being dropped back and having to stay longer than necessary. So I lied to medical and finished boot camp with my platoon, only about 70 of the original 125 recruits finished together. On boot leave I went to the doctor and found out I had full blown Pneumonia.

—**Sgt Andrew Curtis**

Everything in between:

People may find it hard to believe but I had a difficult time in boot camp. My fear of making mistakes and ending up on the quarter deck made me into a neurotic person with tendencies I don't think ever really went away. When a healthy fear should have consumed my being, all that was there was nervousness about how well I could perform a task and not end up on the quarter deck. This thinking consumed my every fiber which is ridiculous because we were IT'd, or as they say in Parris Island, "smoked", everyday regardless of what we did. I had that lottery ticket's buyer mentality that maybe it was possible not to be smoked every day and if we did everything perfect there was no way they could smoke us. But I was so young and naïve. This thinking was all that was in my head, every day, every night, and even in my dreams. I was told I would scream out, "BY YOUR LEAVE SIR, GOOD AFTERNOON SIR!" in my sleep, but I never knew for sure if I did. To make life better about three weeks into boot camp we got a new Drill Instructor named Sgt Ayers. Appropriate name enough as Ayers sounds like Ares, the Greek God of War.

Sgt Ayers, our own Cuban God of War, sent down from the heavens blessing us with his knowledge of battle and here to train us into perfect killers! From week three and on we were graced with his awe inspiring presence as he drilled into us more discipline than was necessary, but the results spoke for themselves as we won all five of the much coveted trophies! When he walked in a hurry, he looked like he could walk through a wall and not notice it was there. His hands would flail as if they had no bones in them but his arms were stiff as rods. He spoke with a very distinct deep growl that was a mix of a bullfrog and pitbull. Yet when we heard him speak the last day of boot camp he sounded like a child whose balls had not dropped yet.

A wrong look would send you to the quarter deck. A weak response would send you there. A step out of place meant your life was over. There was no flying under his radar because if there ever was a super human with extra heightened senses bordering on mutant powers, he was surely it. He once saw someone blink while his back was to him. He could tell when our eyes closed as we laid down in our racks before we slept while we waited for the command to sleep in the dark. He could see down to the atomic level as he would always find space between our elbows and our bodies at the position of attention. He was no mere mortal and he was far above a normal Drill Instructor. His look spoke volumes and if he walked pass you without noticing you, it was as if God had directly intervened with your life right then and there. There were many atheists before he joined us but soon after he joined us, we were all God fearing men. He used to tell us, "As I walk through the Valley of the Shadow of Death, I fear no evil because I am the baddest motherfucker down there". I never knew any to freely edit the bible the way he did but when he spoke, we listened as if it were original text.

There were many like him but he was ours. He put us through hell and we hated every moment we spent with him, but after we left, we realized we missed it. Not many people can truly say they encountered a human force of nature, but if there was one he was surely it.

I would like to say I handled boot camp like a champ, like I came onto that island as some type of fierce beast only being tamed because I allowed it. But that wasn't the case; they broke me. I had thought before I went in that I would find the right answers, be the quickest, the strongest, and the toughest right at the perfect times but that wasn't the case. I failed epically numerous times and not only did I make failure look like a work of art, but I did it to the point where I thought no other outcome was possible. Through the weeks, this hell was burnt into me and I accepted it not because it was something I loved but only because I was trying to survive. I embraced this fire so much that the Drill Instructors were impressed by it. They thought I was trying to be a Marine, but I was just trying to survive; chow by chow, Sunday by Sunday. The only things that kept me going were letters and knowing that this could not possibly last forever, even though at times it seemed like it would. And as much as I thought I was suffering, when recruits started to cry, I didn't. I realized that this personal hell of mine was not so personal and that everyone that was there was experiencing it with me.

When a person digs, sometimes, shovel after shovel, the soil just comes up somewhat easily. Other times you dig and find nothing but hard rock after a few shovels. They dug as far as they could with me, but I had no more suffering to give, so when people needed a hand, I was the rock upon which they stood. What was funny about it was I never saw this foundation coming from anywhere else but besides myself until after it was all done. I thought I was special because of who I was and what I was going through. I was nothing though. I was special because of the people around me. Those people gave me strength, and the pain that was driven into me made me into steel. I would try to be strong for those around me and the people around me were strong for me. Alone I was weak but with them I was unbreakable. Those thirteen and a half weeks forged a weapon that the world has seen time and time again, but only those who have been through it recognize the sharpness of that blade. I was only a small part of that weapon, but that weapon made me all I am. They had forged us into something that would seem so recognizable to so many, but different from everything else. There are only a few like us. We will never change, and it will always be a part of us. When things get hard I don't need to look at what I am because I already know. I see the strength that is inside of me and I laugh when people who don't know this way say life is hard. I laugh because I know who I am and what I will always be; a United States Marine.

In the past we were known as Spartans. Afterwards we conquered lands where we did not know the language as Legionnaires. History would remember us later as Templar's. Today we can be recognized by our Eagle, Globe, and Anchor. Waves have crashed, nights have passed, and stars dot the skies, but some things never change. We have always been here, and always will be. When people call for peace, we will be that weapon of war. This is the way it is and always has been. We would have it no other way.

—Sgt Ian Hernandez

The other side:

Life of a Drill Instructor is very challenging with long hours, little sleep, no food. 12 straight weeks of work

A typical day for a Drill Instructor: The day starts at 4:30 in the morning, with reveille waking up the recruits, then doing a head count to make sure we have all the recruits, using the head (bathroom), and getting recruits dressed. Now all this happens in less than 10 minutes.

Next we march the recruits to chow to eat, after a quick breakfast, Drill Instructors march the recruits back to the squad bays where recruits live and use the head again and clean the house. The day has begun, and the training schedule will dictate what goes on the rest of the day. Some standard training events: Physical Training -running, pull-ups, crunches-, learning Drill - marching, and Marine Corp history.

The day normally ends with evening chow, followed by recruits cleaning house again, square away time when recruits shower, shave, receive mail, and write mail. Recruits go to sleep around 2100 (9:00 pm), while Drill Instructors go and prepare for the next day.

The hardest part of the job is of course the long hours, Drill

Instructors normal work 18-20 hours every day. The body never gets used to it. The best or most rewarding part as a Drill Instructor is graduating a platoon of recruits. Just seeing the families' reactions to all the changes and improvements they see that their son has made in becoming a Marine. Parents and family member come up and shake your hand and thank you for what Drill Instructors do, it is very rewarding.

As for social life, Drill Instructor do not have one while they are training recruits. In between cycles or breaks between pla toons, normally two weeks, is when Drill Instructors try to catch up with everything that they missed.

As far as funny stories are concerned that depends on what you find funny. Recruits say and do some of the stupidest things. Many times DIs have to hide their faces in order not to lose their bearing. I've seen recruits pee themselves, shit their pants, and throw up on each other. Recruits reactions to the experience of the gas chamber can be quit humorous as well.

It was one of the greatest experiences of my life. I learned a lot about myself and pushed my body and mind to extents I never thought were possible. The experience of being a Drill Instructor enhanced my development as a Marine, a leader, and as a person.

—GySgt Rob Browning

The physicals at MEPs failed miserably on one occasion.

I had a recruit on the quarterdeck and I was making him do the standard shit, pushups, mountain climbers, the whole thing. And then… he dies.

The whole thing kind of blurs together from there as you're trying to perform CPR and get him to a professional facility, but long story short, he had a heart condition the doctors performing the physicals at MEPs missed. He never should've been there.

You have a little bit of time away and spend some time blaming yourself, bad luck and eventually just settle on it being someone else's fault. Because it was,

I realized I had a job to do… and that's all I was doing.

I came back a few days later. The platoon hadn't seen me since. I stepped immediately onto the quarter, yelled, "Zero!" and "Ears!" and then asked, "Alright, who am I gonna kill next?"

The job is to make rough men. We excel at our jobs.

—Anonymous

On the first day…

Bequet was my battle buddy and the sun hadn't come up yet. I had to attempt to fireman carry him across a log surrounded by water. That's like a fireman carrying someone from a fire only this was across a log floating on water. By 0400 I was sopping wet and freezing my ass off. Not a good start to the Crucible…

The Sun was up a bit.

The challenge consisted of four boxes in a baseball diamond formation including a tall pole in the middle. Attached at the top of the pole was a rope that dangled down just long enough to reach each box. It looked like the Marine Corp version of Tetherball. We were the ball…

Everyone lined up behind the first box, rifles slung across our backs. There was a line drawn in the sand that we couldn't cross which intersected the first box. Getting on the box was our only option. And we had to get the rope that was dangling lifeless in the middle. We leaned one recruit over the edge of the first box with a rifle extended in his left hand as we held on to his right leg and arm, gently easing him to the rope to snatch it. This was no normal rope. Whatever rope the Marine Corp used to lift heavy shit with, this is the rope they used. Plus, it had a giant knot at the end.

The objective was to get everyone from the line at the first box (home plate), to the other boxes in sequential order, then back to the line (home plate). We begin. The first recruit swings and

212

lands on box two (first base), then whips the rope back to the recruit standing on box one (home plate). That recruit swings to the box two (first base) and gets caught by the recruit standing there. The ballet continues on…

My turn.

I made it to box 4 (third base) and was looking at "home plate" The rope was being swung back around to me. The recruit next to me on the box lost his balance as he was trying to get out of the way for me to catch the rope, instinctually I turned towards him. In slow motion he fell off and I caught what felt like Thor's hammer square in my nuts.

Off the box we both went.

The only way to describe what happens next is to visualize a bunch of guys standing in a circle watching another guy get hit in the balls, really fucking hard.

All I remember is a Humvee medical unit pull up. The corpsmen asked if I was able to continue training. I was still in the fetal position cupping my balls. I requested a moment to rest. The medic told me to go sit in the port-o-potty until I felt better, or discontinue training. I knew if I stopped training now I would get "sent back".

I went to the Port-o-potty and massaged my nuts and made the fastest nut shot recovery of all time.

While in the port-o-potty I did laugh out loud, between tears, thinking of how I would explain getting "sent back" to another platoon DI. "COULDN'T PROTECT MY BALLS SIR!"

Get out of this smelly port o potty and get back out there.

Fire-watch usually means you just lose sleep but when you want desert, adapt and overcome. We knew there were half eaten MRE's in the dumpster. We weren't allowed to have any of the sweet treats that came along with our MRE's so they all got tossed. When it's 4am your cold, bored, and hungry, your damn right I'll dig through that.

You have limited options when you find a bag of coco mix and no hot water. Eat it straight! I had chewed tobacco a few times in high school. But when you put a pinch of chaw that's pure MRE chocolate powder mix in your gums, it's heaven. Willy Wonka couldn't' think of a better confection. After our discovery of delight, me and Walls, our new guide, strategized our fire watch and we traded off running to the dumpsters every night to dig through the trash and bring it back the powdery delights. It was risky but worth every morsel.

Towards the end of boot camp there were a lot of emotions. The first was the physical pain of DI Jameson putting my mosquito wings directly into my collar bones. The second was getting the eagle, globe and anchor. I always imagined my parents sitting next to Pat's parents and after we were respectable Marines we could justify all the crazy shit we did pre Marine Corp.

Rand and I had friendship transplant feelings from what Pat and he had, because he knew we were friends. The last week was kind KINDA fun. Rand had me ride in his POV to move some desks and chairs around MCRD. I felt like a king walking around by myself lifting things for him. His truck was awesome, huge tires that screamed I'm bigger faster and badder than you, and Rand in the driver's seat. I CANT WAIT TO TELL PAT ABOUT THIS HES GOING TO BE SO JEALOUS!

The next day…

Rand calls me to the Duty Hut. "Swim qual 1 hey? Fish, eh? Want to go Recon 0321?! Good to go, go get me some sugar for my coffee killer."

I stared stunned and confused.

"Don't think, go!" he says   Oh God this is awesome! My first sanctioned mission as an almost Marine!

Blend in to other recruits, Get near the ones with the high and tights, ."Early chow, sir!"

"GET SOME!"

"GET SOME AYE AYE SIR!" Shuffle through the line, acquire unnecessary egg formula with anti-boner formula mixed in it to look like a normal breakfast, shuffle to condiments, sugar packets... HERE WE GO! Shit! Regular or sweet and low?... BOTH! Gingerly move fist full of sugar to left pocket aaaaand we're good ...Wait a tick... Drill instructor Staff Sergeant Rand may like a doughnut with his coffee. And there she goes in a napkin into my cammie blouse. Exit Chow Hall.

Re- enter squad bay and knock on DI Duty Hut requesting permission to speak with DI SSGT Rand. OH SHIT, all three of them are fucking inside the Duty Hut?! Rand was looking over my shoulder expecting to see another DI dragging me in by my ear lobe I guess. But according to his ear to ear grin after seeing my sugar and doughnut dump on his desk I guess he was happy with me. "MISSION ACCOMPLISHED AYE AYE SIR!" I said with the most satisfactory voice I've ever had in my life.

Immediately after...

Victories are short if non-existent in USMC boot camp..."So you were a cop, hey Bruckner?"

" No sir. Dispatcher, sir!"

Rand sat with what I assumed to be my file in his lap. "Where at?"

"Elm Grove, WI sir, its near...."

"SHUT THE FUCK UP! I know exactly where it is. You gave me a goddamn speeding ticket while I drove through your shitty town."

"This recruit..."

"SHUT THE FUCK UP. GET OUT!"

Holy Fuck...thank god he didn't take the time to read my file the first day of boot camp...If the past three months were shitty, imagine being able to fuck with the dipshit kid that had something to do with a speeding ticket you got?! I was reminded in

215

that moment, no matter what mission, job, task etc you get in the Marine Corps you will never get a "thank you". If you do something right, you were already expected to. You were a Marine.

A day or two later and the last afternoon at boot camp:

I always wondered why there was a baseball field in the middle of MCRD. The first week or so at boot camp when I saw it I imagined Sundays off and playing ball with the platoon etc…just like in the WWII films….not at all our reality. What I came to find out is that's where the DI's go the last day, play ball get hammered. And they did. They came back to the squad bay having "team week" recruits deliver all of the boxes with our civvies from day one.

"Get online!"

We all do, with pep. "Create the catwalk!"

We looked at each other nervously. Someone yelled, "Create the catwalk, aye-aye sir!"…that was funny. So programmed… What the fuck is a catwalk? I mean honestly the first thing I thought of was that song "I'm too sexy", but since the Marine Corps has weird names for everything like "go fasters", "ink stick", etc. who knows what a Marine Corps "catwalk" was…

I was right…

"THIS! A FUCKING CATWALK!" as Rand began dragging the first few footlockers from in front of our racks, aligning them in a row down the "DI highway".

Then we saw Kebler walk in with a mini multi colored disco strobe light and a boom box, I thought, Christ! What kind of test is this! We graduate tomorrow! But by that time you just expected to get fucked with. The rest of us complied and built our first ever "catwalk." 60 some odd footlockers in a row.

"Open your boxes and put your civvies on! YOU HAVE, 10 9 8 7…" the boom box and strobe got turned on and the squad bay lights went out. It must have taken 15min for us to get in our civvies we were laughing so hard at each other. "Nasty civilian!"

was being yelled left and right at each other laughingly. Nobody's pants fit since we had all lost so much weight, old t-shirts still drenched in the fear that soaked into them on the first day. We had transformed into the cleanest cut, proudest men on the planet to "gansta lookin" thugs dancing around with a strobe light in the background just starting to remember our humanity. The DI's just sat in their chairs at the quarter deck and admired their creations.

But that wasn't it. Marines compete.

"OK OK... Get online nasties." Then the catwalk was activated. As we were all numbered in rack order, we followed one after the other and took one step up on the end of the catwalk and did our best Cindy Crawford walk. The entire platoon hooted and hollered along with the DI's. Most held their pants up with their hands, others had their belts so tight that they looked like MC Hammer. I don't remember who won "best in show," but I feel like we all did in that moment.

We're on the range practicing for qualification... Finally

Pat gets pulled off the line...Unexpected

Continue to fire without someone to my left to compete with... Confused

Commotion to the rear...Worried

Put rifle on safe and look to rear...Disbelief

It was Pat.

My mind cleared. The drill instructors had cleared my rifle. Pat was gone. Drill Instructor Staff Sergeant Jameson pulled me out of the squad bay. We went into "the bubble". That bubble filled with tears as I learned of what happened. Pat's dad was dead and Pat was gone. DI Jameson left me outside for a moment to compose myself. I returned to the squad bay trying to avert my eyes from the spot where spot where Pat was supposed to be, posting as usual. Time and space weren't operating as normal but muscle memory called my body to action when I heard Drill Instructor Staff Sergeant Kebler roar, "Recruit Bruckner!" and the platoon responded as usual, "Recruit Bruckner, aye-aye sir!" I ran to the Drill Instructor Hut. "Recruit Bruckner reporting as ordered Sir!"

"Get in here."

"Get in here, aye-aye sir!"

If I was allowed to shit on Marine Corp time, that would have been swell. But not even fear qualifies as a reason. Kebler slammed the Duty Hut door shut and was within arm's length. He gave me a peculiar look and asked me if I was "Okay.".I said, "Yes, sir," in a monotone voice. He slammed his wall locker and kicked some other stuff around to make noise. The impression of him kicking my ass for being outside while the platoon was inside helped me save face. "Holy Shit he's human."

—Derek Bruckner

"Semper Fi"

"Semper Fidelis"

The Marine Corps adopted the motto *"Semper Fidelis"* in 1883. Prior to that date three mottoes, all traditional rather than official, were used. The first of these, antedating the War of 1812, was *"Fortitudine."* The Latin phrase for "with courage," it was emblazoned on the brass shako plates worn by Marines during the Federal period. The second motto was "By Sea and by Land," taken from the British Royal Marines "Per Mare, Per Terram." Until 1848, the third motto was "To the shores of Tripoli." Inscribed on the Marine Corps colors, this commemorated Presley O'Bannon's capture of the city of Derna in 1805. In 1848, this was revised to "From the halls of the Montezumas to the shores of Tripoli."

"Semper Fidelis" signifies the dedication that individual Marines have to "Corps and country," and to their fellow Marines. It is a way of life. Said one former Marine, "It is not negotiable. It is not relative, but absolute...Marines pride themselves on their mission and steadfast dedication to accomplish it."

Courtesy—U.S. Marine Corps Museum

The Marines' Hymn

Following the Barbary Wars of 1805, the Colors of the Corps were inscribed with the words "to the shores of Tripoli." After the capture and occupation of Mexico City in 1847, the Colors were changed to read "from the shores of Tripoli to the Halls of Montezuma." These events in Marine Corps history are the origin of the opening words of the Marines' Hymn.

Tradition holds that the words to the Marines' Hymn were written by a Marine serving in Mexico. In truth, the author of the words remains unknown. Colonel Albert S. McLemore and Walter F. Smith, Assistant Band Director during the John Philip Sousa era, sought to trace the melody to its origins. It was reported to Colonel McLemore that by 1878 the tune was very popular in Paris, originally appearing as an aria in the Jacques Offenbach opera Genevieve de Brabant. John Philips Sousa later confirmed this belief in a letter to Major Harold Wirgman, USMC, stating "The melody of the "Halls of Montezuma' is taken from Offenbach's comic opera..."

Its origins notwithstanding, the hymn saw widespread use by the mid-1800s. Copyright ownership of the hymn was given to the Marine Corps per certificate of registration dated 19 August 1891. In 1929, it became the official hymn of the United States Marine Corps with the following verses:

From the Halls of Montezuma
to the Shores of Tripoli,
We fight our country's battles
On the land as on the sea.
First to fight for right and freedom,
And to keep our honor clean,
We are proud to claim the title
of United States Marine.

"Our flag's unfurl'd to every breeze
From dawn to setting sun;
We have fought in every clime and place
Where we could take a gun.
In the snow of far-off northern lands
And in sunny tropic scenes,
You will find us always on the job
The United States Marines.

"Here's health to you and to our Corps
Which we are proud to serve;
In many a strife we've fought for life
And never lost our nerve.
If the Army and the Navy
Ever look on Heaven's scenes,
They will find the streets are guarded
By United States Marines."

On 21 November 1942, the Commandant of the Marine Corps authorized an official change in the first verse, fourth line, to reflect the changing mission of the Marine Corps. The new line read "in the air, on land and sea." That change was originally proposed by Gunnery Sergeant H.L. Tallman, an aviator and veteran of World War I.

Shortly after World War II, Marines began to stand at attention during the playing of The Marines' Hymn, Today that tradition continues today to honor all those who have earned the title "United States Marine."

Courtesy—U.S. Marine Corps Museum

The Eagle, Globe and Anchor

The origins of the eagle, globe, and anchor insignia worn by Marines can be traced to those ornaments worn by early Continental Marines as well as to the British Royal Marines.

In 1776, Marines wore a device depicting a fouled anchor. Changes were made to that device in 1798, 1821, and 1824. An eagle was added in 1834. The current insignia dates to 1868 when Brigadier General Commandant Jacob Zeilin convened a board "to decide and report upon the various devices of cap ornaments of the Marine Corps." A new insignia was recommended and approved by the Commandant. On 19 November 1868, the new insignia was accepted by the Secretary of the Navy.

The new emblem featured a globe showing the western hemisphere intersected by a fouled anchor and surmounted by an eagle. Atop the device, a ribbon was inscribed with the Latin motto "Semper Fidelis." The globe signified the service of the United States Marines throughout the world. The anchor was indicative of the amphibious nature of the Marine Corps. The eagle, symbolizing a proud nation, was not the American bald eagle, but rather a crested eagle, a species found throughout the world.

On 22 June 1954, President Dwight D. Eisenhower signed an Executive Order which approved the design of an official seal for the United States Marine Corps. Designed at the request of General Lemuel C. Shepherd, Jr., Commandant of the Marine Corps, the seal replaced the crested eagle with the American bald eagle, its wings proudly displayed. With the approval of this seal by the President of the United States in 1955, the emblem centered on the seal was adopted as the official Marine Corps emblem.

The eagle, globe, and anchor insignia is a testament to the training of the individual Marine, to the history and traditions of the Marine Corps, and to the values upheld by the Corps. It represents "those intangible possessions that cannot be issued: pride, honor, integrity, and being able to carry on the traditions for generations of warriors past." Said retired Sergeant Major David W. Sommers, "the emblem of the Corps is the common thread that binds all Marines together, officer and enlisted, past and present...The eagle, globe and anchor tells the world who we are, what we stand for, and what we are capable of, in a single glance."

Courtesy—U.S. Marine Corps Museum

"RIP Cpl Eric Towner (1981-2005).
The world was a brighter place for us with you in it.
I only wish you had seen that, too."